Playing Black Cheap

Playing Black Cheap

To see this flag in color and order it go online to:
http://asetbooks.com/Us/Mall/Blackidentityitems.html

Playing Black Cheap

INCLUDES THE FOLLOWING:

"Playing Black Cheap: Are African-Americans Taking Too Much For Granted?"

"Jew Yesterday / African-American Tomorrow: Are African-Americans Prepared To Prevent Another Holocaust?"

"The Vote: Friend or Foe of Black People?"

"Europe: White America's Roots! Should Black People Really Want to Integrate With White People?"

"Is Integrating With White People A Healthy Solution"

"On the Way to the Nuthouse"

Final Words

FOREWORD

We, Black People, play Ourselves cheap in so many ways. We need to take a closer look at Ourselves, individually and collectively, and make Ourselves more aware of Our subconscious tendency to play Ourselves cheap. Simply by becoming more aware of the fact that We do it, We can develop the ability to short-circuit it.

If We can begin to short-circuit that tendency, We can begin to project different images of Black People to Ourselves and others throughout the world. This, in turn, would enable Us to project a positive Black reality into the minds and instincts of Black People and others throughout the world.

PLAYING BLACK CHEAP is a political evaluation of a manner of thought and conduct that has critical and far-reaching implications. Damaging behaviors of the most subliminal type at the most personal levels of human intercourse have invaded Our essence, settled in and asserted themselves, promoting images and impressions that are self-negating and menacing to Our well-being.

We play Black People cheap collectively when We act as if Black People are handicapped in a way or to a degree that differs from that of other groups of people (particularly white people). And We play Black People cheap as individuals when We act as if the efforts of individual Blacks who are independent-minded do not deserve to be taken seriously or accorded the same level of consideration as the proclamations of individual whites and other proponents of white perspectives.

When We play Black People cheap as individuals, independent-minded Blacks are not able to make as great an impact in the Black community as they should make. They are rendered less likely to broadly influence the development of Black People and the course of human events. When We play Black People cheap as a race, We make it easy for white power to dominate world affairs and determine what the future of Black People will be. That is the most damaging wrong because the future of Black People should not be disproportionately impacted on by non-Black parties.

Black People in the United States who play Black cheap are taking too much for granted. In the long run, little that is good will come from that. However, a great deal that is good will come when Black individuals reach inside and take on more personal responsibility for Our development as a people.

Mba Mbulu July, 2000

Table Of Contents

Mba Mbulu's Ebooks and PaperBack Books

PLAYING BLACK CHEAP: Are African Americans Taking Too Much For Granted?

"When in a white power environment, intelligent people prepare for the worst."

Playing Black Cheap:
Are African Americans Taking Too Much For Granted?

Black People are playing Black cheap today, and We are going to pay the price in the near future!

Black men and women play Black cheap more than any other group of people, including white racists. We play Black cheap because We constantly make large and small decisions that reveal a preference for satisfying white expectations instead of Black ones. Every day We make large and small decisions that identify Us as white sympathizers, not Black ones. I will be attacked for stating what is so obvious, but millions of Black individuals, especially those who have encountered a degree of "success," would rather identify with "white" than "Black."

Millions of Black men and women, especially those who have encountered a degree of "success," will pay a lot of money and go through all sorts of humiliations to obtain a white stamp of approval, but they don't value a Black-centric stamp of approval at all. Black men and women will sacrifice to purchase and display certain white-authored books, but they act like Black-authored books are not worthy of their hard earned money. Black men and women will rake and scrape to pay for a mainstream speaker or white instructor, but a Black speaker or instructor is expected to come free of charge or for a pittance. Black individuals want to be mainstream, but act like they don't know the mainstream in the United States does not give a damn about Black People.

Since the mainstream doesn't give a damn about Black People, Black individuals who are overly concerned about mainstream impressions and priorities tend to play Black cheap. Sometimes, they do so in order to de-emphasize their non-mainstream appearance. Since their Black skin boldly announces who they are and what they should be about, they have to act in a manner that quickly neutralizes the conclusions their significant others- white people- are apt to "jump to." At other times, they do so in order to emphasize the fact that they are "independent" thinkers as opposed to "Black" thinkers, and members of the human race, not members of the "Black" race. And at still other times, they do so because they are politically ignorant and poorly informed to the point that they fail to recognize the importance of being Black and proud, and acting in the interest of Black People. As such, they not only harm themselves, they help cripple Black People and set Blacks up for a rude awakening.

Are African-Americans taking too much for granted? Considering the history of white-Black relations in the United States of America, of the physical harm inflicted on Our minds and bodies and immeasurable scars rammed into Our spirit and psyche, should African-Americans be as trusting of white people as they are? The answer is obviously "No!" but the same is true of a battered woman who keeps returning to the man who abuses her. When analyzing white-Black relations in the United States, Black People must be seen as playing a role analogous to that of the battered woman, the disconcerted battered woman. Are We, like the disconcerted battered woman, incapable of making the decision that will ensure Our safety and promote the well being of Our people?

The question must be asked over and over, "Are African-Americans taking too much for granted?" "Are African-Americans making safe decisions, decisions that will be good for Black People in the short and long runs?" Are African-Americans recognizing that Black People are the only reliable source of salvation for Us, and are African-Americans using that recognition to err on the side of caution? If African-Americans err, if African-Americans err at all, it must be on the side of caution. A bad decision made as a consequence of political naivete, childlike innocence or irresponsibleness is likely to be just as damaging as any other bad decision. Therefore, it is best that African-Americans err on the side of caution. It is best that Black People be prepared to defend Black People. That way, if a worse case scenario should present itself, Black People will not suffer disproportionately.

Ignore reality, if you consciously or subconsciously choose to do so. Concentrate on conditions you want to exist instead of those that actually exist, if you are naive enough to think that is the best approach. Rely on your historical enemy to "treat" you right, if you have been convinced that your destiny and your enemy's destiny are one and the same. But when the dire consequences of your responses take their toll, don't cop a plea or come up with excuses because that will not undo the damage you will have caused. When you play Black People cheap what you have committed is a serious indiscretion.

JEW YESTERDAY/ AFRICAN-AMERICAN TOMORROW:

Are African-Americans Prepared to Prevent Another Holocaust?

PLAYING BLACK CHEAP

Jew Yesterday/ African-American Tomorrow?

Are African Americans Prepared To Prevent Another Holocaust?

INTRODUCTION

The story of the Jews is well known; the Bible has made many of us somewhat aware of what took place. We will briefly review the story of their development and state clearly what the Bible only hints at.

At about 1800 BC twelve families (about 70 persons in all) left a section of west Asia near present day Palestine because of famine/hunger, and settled on the outskirts of a great Black empire in Egypt. The population of Egypt warmly accepted these nomads and helped them survive by employing them in various capacities. As time passed this group's numbers became larger and larger, so the Egyptians began to view them as a security risk, fearing the whites would plot against them if they were attacked by foreigners. As a result, the Egyptians began to place restrictions on the shepherds (whites call this "persecution"). This "persecution" continued until a Black "Jew" named Moses came up with a religion that he used to lead his people, now 600,000 strong, to what he called the "promised land." They attacked the people who owned that land, took it from them, occupied it and called it their homeland.

Not long after the Jews had taken the promised land they lost grasp of their religion. They felt they didn't need it anymore because they were no longer in fear of being persecuted by the Egyptians. The unity that this religion had created among them went as the religion went, and the Jews began to scatter to all parts of the world.

Wherever the Jews settled, they were primarily

concerned about two things: one was economic and material security, which they had always lacked, and the other was a fear of being massacred by the people surrounding them. This fear of being massacred, like all political realities, had a historical basis. The Jews had always been nomads and never organized themselves against attacks. Since they were constantly following their sheep they were constantly running into hostile tribes that made war on them. Once they became a threat to the Egyptians they realized how easily the powerful Egyptians could destroy them, and lived with this fear for hundreds of years. After so long a period, this fear became a part of their psyche, their social make-up. The Jews thought both of these problems were solved when western white people began to dominate the world, not long before the proclaimed birth of Jesus.

The Jews entered into the economic world of the western whites, and their business smarts and thirst for profits enabled them to prosper and dominate many economic areas and activities. This prosperity relieved them of many economic concerns and greatly reduced their fear of being massacred. Still they were a despised and politically powerless people (despised because they were "Semites," and politically powerless because they lived and prospered in countries that were controlled by non-Jews), but they could not be convinced that the whites would take extreme political measures against them. They preferred to think that the dominant white societies had accepted them as brothers and ignored all of the evidence to the contrary.

In the 1400s of the present era, the whites in the western European countries reminded the Jews of how despised and powerless they were. Throughout Europe during this time period, the Jews were systematically persecuted far more than the Egyptians had ever done. In the 1490s, the Spanish whites decided to rid themselves of the Jews altogether, and expelled them from Spain. Other European governments wanted to do likewise, but did not want to enact a law that would serve that purpose. Most chose to persecute the Jews so much that they would voluntarily leave en masse, but the Jews were either not smart enough to get the message or too dumb to independently act in their own interest. They chose to remain in these hostile countries, unwilling to organize around their Jewish essence and unable to defend themselves against the economic and political whims of hostile people.

Slightly more than 400 years later, on the eve of World War II, Adolf Hitler, Chancellor of Germany, doing what many western whites wanted to do, initiated extreme political measures against the Jews. With the assistance of millions of whites in Germany, Hitler ordered that Jews be transported to concentration camps and executed. This relit the ancient Jewish fear of being exterminated and led them to demand a homeland of their own. The British, anxious to relieve themselves of the Jews in Britain, played the role of Jehovah and promised the Jews some land that was already occupied by other people. The British first offered the Jews the African country of Uganda, but the Jews rejected that location. Then the Jews were offered a location not far from their ancient homeland. The Jews accepted that offer, the location was ridded of its present inhabitants, the Jews named their new country Israel and settled down in the midst of the people they had robbed of their homeland.

Throughout modern history, the Jews played themselves cheap. They found out how costly that can be. However, the path they walked leading up to the eve of World War II is, in many regards, being mimicked by African-Americans. Are some cruel elements of the

Jewish past in the future of the African-American? Time will tell.

EERIE SIMILARITIES

Guess what happened in 1871!! Civil rights for Jews were written into the German constitution. In 1933, 62 years later, the Jews were marching, stupor-like, into concentration camps and being exterminated. The Jews didn't realize it at the time, but civil rights made it easy for them to play themselves cheap. They played themselves cheap, and if what people are taught is true, they paid an expensive price.

Guess what happened in 1964!! Civil rights legislation specifically designed to benefit African-Americans was made part of the law of the United States of America. It is now 35 years later. Materially speaking, the statistics clearly demonstrate that African-Americans continue to lose ground. But what is frightening is that African-Americans have lost the image of themselves as a distinct group of people and play themselves cheap as if it were the natural thing to do. This is in sharp contrast to the Blacks who lived prior to the civil rights era.

If one looks where African-Americans are 35 years after being granted civil rights, and compares that to where the Jews were 62 years after being granted civil rights, one has to be somewhat alarmed.

Sixty to seventy years is the equivalent of three human generations. If We begin slightly before the civil rights period in Germany, We will see that the first generation of Jews fought for civil rights, brought it about and enjoyed some of its "rewards." The second generation dived heart and soul into "integration," downplayed the essence of their Jewishness, defined themselves within a mainstream context and enjoyed even more of integration's "rewards." The third generation of Jews knew not what it was, mistook appearances for reality, and almost fixated on the importance of being "good" German citizens. But most "good" German citizens despised Jews and co-operated with authorities who had hatched a plan to do away with them. By the time the Jews snapped out of their stupor, the holocaust had exterminated or ruined millions of them and was cruelly engraved into the psyche of all of them.

Neither the Jews nor the Germans realized it at the time, but civil rights was an early step toward a human nightmare. The Jews didn't have to experience that nightmare, but what they wanted to be happening carried more weight than what was actually happening. In the long run reality prevailed (as it always does) and the Jews paid the political price that foolish groups of people tend to pay.

Ignore reality, if you have been trained to do so. Concentrate on what you want to exist instead of what actually exists, if you have been made confident that that is the best approach. Rely on your historical enemy to "treat" you right, if you have been convinced that your destiny and your enemy's destiny are one and the same. But don't expect your enemies to be affected by your wants, and don't expect the victims, your victims, to conclude that you meant them no harm.

The Jews victimized themselves; that is, they acted in a manner that made them disproportionately vulnerable and easy to abuse. Let Us observe a few of the steps that stood out in this process. I will refer to Michael Brenner, a Jewish Professor of Jewish History and Culture at the University of Munich [Germany]. Mr. Brenner made some interesting revelations in a book he wrote entitled THE RENAISSANCE OF JEWISH CULTURE IN WEIMAR GERMANY (1996). (For those who may not know, the Weimar years made up the period between World War 1 and World War 2. During these years attempts were made in various European countries to get rid of the Jews.)

(1) Mr. Brenner speaks of Jews who had taken themselves "beyond Judaism," of Jews who "failed to create a particular culture and only contributed to German culture before they were reminded in 1933 of their Jewishness." When Mr. Brenner speaks of Judaism, he is not speaking solely of a religion, but of the essence of the Jewish culture. In the process of moving "beyond Judaism," the Jews moved beyond themselves. They de-prioritized their essence, practically abandoned it in fact, in order to embrace a German essence, a German culture, a German reality. Having been granted civil rights, the Jews abandoned themselves and resolved to melt into the German mainstream, to prove to the Germans that Jews could be just as German as the Germans. But the Jews did not have the power within the system to force this process through to fruition; German ethnocentrism was too powerful to be dominated by Jewish compliance and do-good intentions. The relative weakness of Jewish power within the system was made known to everyone in 1933, when the real Germans reminded the wannabe Germans (Jews) of their differences, put the wannabe Germans "back in their place" and exterminated hundreds of thousands, maybe even millions of them.

Since civil rights was made the law of the United States of America, the number of African-Americans who preach that race is no longer a relevant factor reminds one of the Jews in Europe who were spreading the same type message. Many African-Americans, some with the support of white power dollars and exposure, are advocating that race should be ignored, and they are promoting an image of a white America that is trying to turn all of America into one big, happy family. But no sincere effort to substantially transform America is being made, and African-Americans need to face up to that reality. We already know that the Jews in Weimar Germany failed in that regard. The Jews in Germany failed to face up to reality, so African-Americans should be wary of committing the same failure.

(2) Jews who wanted "culture left Judaism at once, and completely, even though most of them remained conscious of their Jewish origin," Mr. Brenner noted. That is to say, the Jews moved full speed ahead into "integration." As I stated earlier, they wanted to prove their German-worthiness. They were conscious of their Jewishness, but not proud of it, not protective of it, they did not promote its legitimacy; in spite of statements they might have made to the contrary. Civil rights had interfered with their bearings, and they, from a practical standpoint, did not remember from whence they came, where they stood or where they needed to go. As such, Jewish self-definition ceased; the "wannabe German" in them began to do all of the defining. Their expressed hold onto Jewry remained strong, but the fact of the matter was that they had let it slip away. They began to place their essence and culture in a museum, so to speak, instead of expressing and experiencing it in real life ways. An occasional vocal outburst, a demonstrative reaction to a maiming or a civil injustice, a book on a table, a lot of pictures on a lot of walls, certain pieces of attire, some songs at an event, instructive memories indexed and filed away; that is what Jewry became to Weimar era Jews. Eerily, they treated Jewry in much the same way post civil rights African-Americans treat Blackness.

African-Americans distance themselves from anything too Black as speedily as they can, yet insist that they are proud of their heritage. African-Americans run away from Black residential areas, Black speech patterns, Black schools and colleges, Black-centric ideas and ideologies, Black interpretations of events and developments, away from Black independent power, Black traditions, self-definition and self-validation, away from non-white Africa, etc. If they want "culture" or "class," African-Americans, like the Weimar Jews, scamper to the white world and the white value system to get it. African-Americans run away from and de-prioritize their essence, yet insist that they are proud of being Black. Their words sound okay, but their actions tell a different story. Like the Weimar era Jews, African-Americans are letting their Blackness slip away. They are playing Black cheap, in much the same manner those Jews played Jewry cheap. The Jews ran away from themselves and into concentration camps. What are African-Americans running into?

(3) Three generations after German Jews had begun to move "out of the ghetto," "the question of what formed the nature of their Jewishness had become ever more acute... Religion alone, however, proved a fragile basis for self-definition among a highly secularized Jewish population, one that came to disavow most ritual practices of Judaism" [Brenner].

I have already explained Judaism as more than a religion; Judaism was the essence of being a Jew. The above quote alerts Us to the evolution of self doubt, a devaluation of self and a loss of self-contact. In short, the Jews were no longer proud of or sure of "what formed the nature of their Jewishness." By the third generation after "integration," the Jews were so unstable that they were unsure of who they were. If We pay attention to the terms "self-definition" and "secularized," We will discover the source of this instability and uncertainty.

The Jews, that is the German wannabes, wanted to create a new form of Judaism; they wanted to give Judaism a new content and essence. Why? Because they had become secularized. Secular is a term that refers to that which is not religious, but We must recognize the secular/religious duality as representative of a much deeper dynamic. Thus, by becoming secularized, the Jews actually had begun to take on the same values as real Germans, not just in religious regards but culturally as well. The third generation Jews wanted a Judaism that they could feel comfortable with as "integrated" German citizens. That desire was the motor that powered their ill-fated thrust toward integration (and the holocaust). But their logic was upside down. Instead of wanting a Judaism that they could feel comfortable with as "integrated" German citizens, they should have wanted an integrated Germany that they could feel comfortable with as self-validating Jews. Within the latter, they could have worked toward transforming Germany without leaving themselves defenseless.

But they left themselves defenseless. "An analysis of the changing self-definition within the liberal majority of German Jews reveals a gradual shift from a community of faith to a community of fate and common descent..." [Brenner] From a "community of faith" (Judaism and all that it implies for Jews) to a "community of fate and common descent" (being a good, "integrated" German; affixing the Jewish destiny to the German destiny). Thus, the Jews traded in something real and substantial for a pipe dream, for something idealistic. That is a trade a people without legally recognized power should never make. But African-Americans have already demonstrated a preference for making that trade.

Like the Jews in Weimar Germany, African-

Americans are falling for the secularization card. That is, African-Americans are being lured away from that something special that defines their essence. African-Americans have been lured into the mainstream, taking on the values of white America and affixing the African American destiny to the white American destiny. Like the Jews, African-Americans are abandoning their essence as they try to prove that they can function at a high level within somebody else's scheme of things. That is a cardinal mistake! The Jewish attempt to do this "was brought to an end not by its own weaknesses but by those of the larger society" [Brenner]. No matter how hard they tried, the Jews could not get the cooperation of "the larger society" (white people in Europe, the power holders). The "larger society" is already undoing similar efforts by African-Americans and will continue to do so. The only question is, "What price will African-Americans eventually pay?"

In the arena of power politics, mistakes are always costly. I will, therefore, repeat the last question. "What price will African-Americans eventually pay?"

(4) During the Weimar period, the Jews were creative and productive, but too much of what they created and produced was not relevant to Jewish culture or the building of an independent Jewish power base. Instead, they created and produced what they felt would be acceptable to Germany's status quo. Their objective was to be accepted as Germans, to prove that they were worthy of being Germans; and they sought that end so blindly that they let go of their most precious possession, their essence. They failed to use their creative and productive energies to communicate with themselves and others in meaningful ways about the Jewish reality. This failure loosened the bond that held the Jewish people together, made it easier for them to let go of their essence (the only thing that was capable

of protecting them) and made them more vulnerable to attack.

According to Brenner, the Jews created "secular forms of culture to express their Jewish distinctiveness." Think about that [and review what was said earlier about "secular"]. When one takes into account all of the parameters that are relevant to the Jewish reality in Weimar Germany, one realizes that it would have been impossible to create "secular forms of culture to express their Jewish distinctiveness." But the Jews tried; the Jews tried the impossible. The Jews tried to use mainstream values to represent their non-mainstream reality. The result, quite predictably, was that they left themselves out of their own art, out of their own music and out of their own literature, and professed ideas that made millions of individuals candidates for annihilation! Jewish intellectuals, Jews with German degrees and PhDs and Jewish financial leaders led the Jewish people to the holocaust, and the Jewish masses and Jewish financial leaders failed to support the sector of Jews who advocated self-empowerment. Jewish intellectuals led the march to the holocaust in two stages. We will discuss those stages, and more, in the next section.

THE ROLE OF JEWISH ELITES

Jewish intellectuals, Jews with German degrees and PhDs, and Jewish financial leaders led the Jewish people to the holocaust, and the Jewish masses and Jewish financial leaders failed to support the sector of Jews who advocated self-empowerment. Jewish intellectuals led the march to the holocaust in two stages. In the first stage, they promoted an apologetic view of Judaism that furthered the cause of "integration." In the second stage, they used the arts, literature, music and scholarship not to express their culture or seek autonomy (empowerment), but to create a new Judaism that would fit into a mainstream that had been violently anti-Jewish for more than a thousand years. They were so intent on proving their "worthiness" that they were willing to become an appendage to the mainstream; the Lone Ranger's Tonto, so to speak. These intellectuals were encouraged, either wittingly or unwittingly, by elements of the German status quo. They were educated in German universities, published and promoted by elements of the German media, "successful," projected as the legitimate representatives of the Jewish people and financed by Jewish financial leaders.

Because they were financially comfortable and profit driven, what Jewish intellectuals advocated was music to the ears of Jewish financial leaders. Based on the response of Jewish financial leaders, they were unwilling to threaten their personal wealth or status by advocating the security of a specific group of people (themselves!). Jewish financial leaders seemed unwilling to support an independent Jewish platform that would disturb a business environment that brought them profits. Additionally, Jewish financial leaders did not indicate a willingness to choose between Germany and Judaism; they did not want to choose between a financial environment that rewarded them and a political platform that might ruin their privileges. They eventually discovered that the basis of their financial success was not the German mainstream. They eventually discovered that the rational Jewish sector was not composed of Jewish intellectuals but Jewish "radicals." They eventually discovered that it was not what they wanted to support that mattered but what they needed to support. In failing to address their needs and the needs of the Jewish people in politically real terms when they should have, they rendered themselves unable to effectively defend themselves when the time came to do so.

Evidence that an identical response has consumed the intellectual and financially comfortable elements of the African-American community is extensive to say the least. Integration has produced African-Americans who proudly declare their support of capitalism and defend the processes innate to white power economics. Statements that racism is no longer a crucial factor in the relationship of Blacks and whites in the United States come out of the mouths of prominent African-Americans so frequently that they pass without much ado. African-Americans travel around the globe defending United States policies that are clearly unfair and oppressive. African-American children are all too often educated in white oriented primary schools and colleges, and end up products of an extended white environment, not an essentially Black one. Many of the better known African-American educators are employed by white universities and colleges, and their values resemble those of the Jewish intellectuals that were just discussed. Educational information about Black People, even when written or produced by African-Americans, is done so under the lurking auspices of white interests. The message of African-American intellectuals is "do what is necessary to promote integration and reject those who advocate a policy that is not integrationist in nature." We know what that message delivered to the Jews in Weimar Germany. Given similar prerequisites and similar conditions, can African-Americans afford to assume that a similar outcome is unlikely? Given similar prerequisites and similar conditions, should African-Americans assume that history will not repeat itself? I think that is a very dangerous assumption to make.

But I am certain that the intellectual and financially comfortable elements of the African-American community are aware of that danger. The Jewish financial leaders of Weimar Germany certainly were. Evidence is abundant that many of them transferred large sums of money to banks outside of Germany. They were hoping that, if hostilities broke out, they would have enough forewarning to make a hasty escape and enjoy life in another country. They, thus, deliberately played Russian roulette with their people and sacrificed their people for personal financial rewards and "status." What a low-life bunch of criminals they were! Since many of today's African-Americans are running the same game, since many of today's African-Americans are deliberately playing Russian roulette with the lives of Black People, they too are a low-life bunch of criminals!!

Remember what was said about Jewish creativity during the Weimar period? The Jews failed to use their creative and productive energies to communicate with themselves and others about the Jewish reality in meaningful ways. When anyone takes a peek at what African-Americans are doing with their creative energies, there is no way the argument can be made that they are using their creative and productive energies to communicate with themselves and others about the Black reality in meaningful ways. African-American "creativity" is driven by windy, integrationist ideologies and the promise of personal financial compensation. Consequently, what is projected as Black is a blurred succession of Tontoist sounds and images. The widely marketed books, the stories that are seen on television and performed on mainstream stages, the speakers heard on the radio, the articles and feature stories that appear in African-American and white newspapers and publications--- all represent a dominant integrationist perspective in varying degrees, all are geared toward "the dollar," all are repulsive toward individuals and organizations that champion a Black centric reality for Black People in this part of the world and all are feeding

Black People ideas that could make African-Americans candidates for a catastrophe. As it did to the Jews in Weimar Germany, the failure of the creative sector of the African-American community to deal with the Black reality seriously is loosening the bond that keeps Black People aware of their vulnerability and uniqueness. For white America, the doctor could not have ordered anything better.

A Black power reality, which is what African-Americans should be concentrating on, is not being dealt with at all by African-Americans who are "comfortable." Thus, African-Americans who are comfortable are repeating the role of their Jewish equivalents in Weimar Germany. African-Americans who are famous or "successful," be they athletes, talk show host, novelists, Hollywood stars, etc., are ignoring the reality of Black and white relations in the United States of America and, in so doing, are contributing to the loosening of ties within the Black community. This loosening of ties makes it easier for white power to impose solutions onto Black People that are detrimental to the well-being of Black People. Acting in like manner, Jewish intellectuals and financial leaders delivered the Jews to Germany's concentration camps. African-American intellectuals and financial sycophants are primed to deliver African-Americans to a similar fate. Are We, the Black masses, going to follow the same flawed leadership types the Jewish masses followed? Not if We have any intelligence left!

Think about it! If comfortable African-Americans are unwilling to champion the security of Black People because it will threaten their personal wealth or status, why should the Black masses support them or look up to them? If comfortable African-Americans are unwilling to support an independent Black platform, what sense does it make for the Black masses to support them or look up to them? And, if comfortable African-Americans are unwilling to choose between white power and Black power, what sense does it make for the Black masses to support them or look up to them? They, like their Jewish predecessors, will eventually discover that the basis of their "comfort" is not white America, it is Black America. They, like their Jewish predecessors, will eventually discover that the rational Black sector is not composed of African-American intellectuals but Black "radicals." They, like their Jewish predecessors, will eventually discover that it is not what they want to support that matters, but what they need to support. But best of all, when they eventually discover what they should already know, they will pay the price, not the Black masses. Why?

Because the Black masses do not have to experience the fate of the Jewish masses simply because "comfortable" African-Americans seem primed to experience the fate of the "comfortable" Jews of Weimar Germany.

CONCLUSION

One generation of intellectually flawed individuals initiated a flawed process and saw it take root. A second generation of flawed intellectuals and entrepreneurs reaped the intoxicating but fleeting benefits of that process. A third generation of flawed individuals, and everybody who was rooted in their culture, suffered the dire and lasting consequences of that process. In a nutshell, that is the story of the Jews in Germany. The Jews seemed to be making so much progress in Germany (and the rest of Europe) that they deluded themselves, put all of their marbles into a bag that belonged to non-Jews (the integration bag), frowned at any talk of self-reliance and walked dead into what they now call the Holocaust. Did the Germans trick the Jews? I think not; but if they did it was only to the extent the Jews allowed themselves to be tricked. Did the Jews act in a manner that would be expected of any responsible group of people? No, not at all; particularly in light of the belligerent nature of the Germans and the abusive nature of white power institutions. Did the Jews act wisely but simply became the victims of bizarre developments? Again, my response is "No." The Germans punished the Jews, but only to the extent made possible by the Jews. The Jews were the authors of their own victimization because they did not take on the basic responsibilities that any group of politically mature adults would have taken on. The Jews wanted to take the easy way out. In white power politics, the easy way out is a bright looking path that leads to Hell.

Albert Memmi, a well-known Jewish philosopher, came to the conclusion that self-rejection never solves anything. Memmi was able to determine that his people, the Jews, had rejected themselves. But what is self-rejection, and how does it manifest itself? Does self-rejection have to be readily obvious? Is self rejection as easily recognizable as "black and white?" For Black People in the United States, is self-rejection an open declaration that white people are "better than" Black People? Is self-rejection a crystal clear demonstration of any type, or can self-rejection operate in subtle, subconscious and chameleonic ways? If some Black individuals are willing to leave their welfare in the hands of another group of people, as "successful" Jews were willing to do, can that be evidence of Black self-rejection? If some Black individuals assert that Black People don't need an independent government, as "educated" Jews did, can that be evidence of Black self-rejection?

When the Jews walked dead into Europe's extermination camps, were they in search of integration or were they trying to escape from themselves? When

Black individuals in the United States diligently oppose Black nationalism--- is it because they think integration is a more practical solution, or is it because they feel Black People are incapable of functioning efficiently without white participation, leadership and guidance?

Should Black People turn a deaf ear to the best solution simply because some Black individuals do not like themselves or trust Black People? I don't think so!

The African-American Reality

Present day African-Americans neither possess the wealth nor financial affluence equivalent to that possessed by the Jews in Europe in the 1930s. Present day African-Americans do not occupy positions of power equivalent to the political clout wielded by Europe's Jews leading up to the 1930s. Whereas the Jews controlled certain channels of the communications, media and entertainment industries in Europe in the 1930s, African-Americans of today are merely superfluous appendages to white power's industries. Because of prior efforts put forth by Jews for nearly 500 years, the Jews of Europe in 1930 had the ways and means to educate, feed, clothe, shelter and defend themselves. Present day African-Americans have not constructed or evolved equivalent ways and means. In fact, in every vital regard, African-Americans today are less integral to white power than the Jews in Europe were 70 years ago. And, in every vital regard, African-Americans today are more vulnerable to abuse than the Jews in Europe were 70 years ago. Yet, two facts boldly jump out at an observer: #1-- the Jews were put "back in their place" and gassed and; In spite of that, #2—African-Americans act as if they are not at risk. Somewhere, somebody is failing to analyze and put the pieces together properly.

Somewhere, intellectually flawed individuals of color are coming to flawed conclusions and managing to popularize those conclusions.

There is much in every opinion, train of thought or ideology that is purely theoretical, and therefore debatable. So when different groups of individuals come to different conclusions, it is frustrating but understandable. However, when Black People in the United States go against common sense to the point where they do not accept the proposition that their well being is primarily their responsibility, that is frightening!

Is it better to prepare for a worse case scenario and have to adjust to a best case reality, or to prepare for a best case scenario and have to adjust to a worst case reality? Black People in the United States need to give serious thought to that question because, one day, either I am going to recognize that those who would criticize me are right or those who would criticize me are going to recognize that I am right. If the mistake is mine, I can let my guard down, adjust to the good times and safely march into the future. But if the mistake belongs to those who would criticize me, so-called African-Americans are going to endure an explosion of additional misery and suffering.

Black People in the United States made progress within somebody else's system during America's Reconstruction years (1865-1877). There were Black legislators, Black judges, Black lawyers, a Black governor, Blacks with vice-presidential aspirations, Blacks fraternizing with whites and Blacks using the U.S. constitution to substantiate their "gains." Less than five years later, less than five years after being "included," wielding "power" and benefiting from an "integrated" America, those same Blacks were disenfranchised, hunted down, raped, castrated, lynched and put "back in their place." Since the basic power relationship between Blacks and whites has not changed from that day to the present, what is going to keep white power from putting African-Americans "back in their place" again?

In spite of some appearances to the contrary, two facts remain: #1-- white power is not rooted in principles of equality and justice and #2--white power distrusts and dislikes Black People. How then, can a balanced Black person feel relatively safe as an "integrated" American?

Wanting integration to work is understandable. Blindly pursuing integration is insulting and, at times, genocidal. Additionally, within the white power scheme of things, integration is a basket that is owned and controlled by white power advocates. Why should Black People repeat the mistake of Weimar era Jews and put Our eggs in that basket? We shouldn't, and balanced Black individuals will not. But flawed Black individuals will.

Humankind: Perennially Idling in Neutral

Present day white Americans are quick to point out that they were not around when Black People were enslaved; the implication being that they would not have been party to such an inhumane institution. Of course they are lying-- telling Black People what they think Black People want to hear. White people today, just like white America's founding fathers, are driven by their personal insecurities and the profit motive. White Americans of today would have flowed with the tide if they had been around 200 years ago and, if the technology were present, would have feverishly pushed their products (Black laborers, Black wenches and Black bucks) over the internet.

Present day whites run the "I wasn't alive then"

line because they know there are feeble-minded African-Americans searching for declarations such as that. Such declarations are fuel for flawed Black intellects that insist that the abuse and slaughter of Blacks by whites will not be repeated. "These are different times" and "white people have changed," they will tell you. But the fact of the matter is this: (1) a date change is not a times change and (2) white people have not changed. Human beings, in general, have not changed. The human beings of the year 2000 are identical to the human beings of 1939, 1880, 1783, 1499 or any other time period. Human beings are performing the same basic functions today that they were performing thousands of years ago. Human beings are motivated by the same factors today that motivated them thousands of years ago. Human beings are being controlled by the same basic instincts today that controlled them thousands of years ago, particularly during periods of stress or when difficult decisions have to be made. In short, in all of the areas that count, human beings today are just like human beings of yesterday.

Humankind today is idling in neutral; rocking back and forth but failing to make an essential advance--just like humankind has been doing for thousands of years. There are individuals who would dispute that assertion, just as Jewish integrationists disputed Jewish nationalists in Europe 70 years ago. But humankind's development has been a series of 4 part cycles; three steps forward, two steps backward, two steps forward and three steps backward. At the end of each cycle, humankind is pretty much where it started. That is because humankind has never actually moved. Some individuals move, but the force they generate produces only a small ripple in humankind's ocean because of the activities of those who oppose change. Not long after its creation, the ripple is absorbed by those who oppose change and the old human ocean flows as it has customarily flowed. It is white America's customary manner of behavior that balanced Black persons refuse to ignore. They realize that what looks like progress today could well be just another ripple. That ripple represents one or two steps that have been taken forward; an equal number of steps backward is imminent. Fortunately, Black People can always be prepared for those attempted steps backward if We take a single page from white people's own book on themselves.

The White American Reality

White people know each other better than anybody else knows them, and WHITE PEOPLE DON'T TRUST EACH OTHER!! European history is a diary filled with constant warfare, complex alliances, conniving pleasantries, consistent back stabbings and timely assassinations. The people of the various white nations, including those of the United States of America, grew up together, played together, slept together and conspired together. White people were around each other when food was scarce, when heat was lacking and when the coffers were empty. They were also around each other when food was plentiful, when heat warmed every body and when the coffers were full. Do you know what? They all came to the conclusion that NONE OF THE "OTHER" WHITES WERE TRUSTWORTHY. Thus, if France had to rely on another white nation for whatever reason, the French people WOULD PREPARE FOR THE WORST. The same is true of the Danes, Portuguese, Swedes, English, Germans and all of the others. If the whites are so certain that their own white brothers and sisters are not trustworthy, how can a rational Black person come to a different conclusion?

Black People in the United States have developed a tolerance for Black suffering and Black pain that brings Our humanity into question. Is the dark-white pot at the end of the evasive integrationist rainbow worth the damage Black People must continue to allow white people to inflict on Us? The accumulated suffering and pain Black People have endured year in and year out (because of their "We Shall Overcome" form of resistance) is several times greater than any harm that would have been done to Us during a war for national liberation. In terms of accumulated suffering, white racism has been several times more damaging to Black People than the Holocaust was to the Jews. How much more suffering do certain self-despising African-Americans expect Black People to endure? Is forcing Ourselves onto white people that important to them?

White people and white power systems play Black People as cheaply today as they ever did. The Black dollar purchases as little as it ever did. The Black vote carries as small a stick as it ever did. Black opinions mean as little as they ever did. The Black lifestyle and culture are belittled as much as they ever were, and Black principles are trivialized until they evaporate. But white power's depreciation of everything Black is not surprising. What is surprising is the lack of appreciation We have for Ourselves. What is not acceptable is the degree to which Black People play Black cheap.

When Push Comes to Shove

When push comes to shove, who do you think white power is going to look out for? When resources are limited, threats are plentiful and fear reigns because of uncertainty about what lies ahead, whose interests do you think white power will give priority to? When goods and services have to be conservatively allocated and rationed to maintain vital institutions, will white people be driven by a new sense of justice or the ancient, crude instincts that have dominated them for thousands of years? Given the choice between undesirable, suspect advocates of white power (African-Americans) and familiar, traditional advocates of white superiority, who do you think white power is going to throw its weight and influence behind? When push came to shove in Europe in the 1930s, the "good" white Germans were swamped by the Nazi tide and did little to undermine white power [Nazism]. When push came to shove in Europe in the 1930s, the Jews were caught with their pants down; they were not prepared to defend themselves. When push came to shove in Europe in the 1930s, the Jews walked dead into white power's extermination camps. Who knows when the day of reckoning will appear on America's landscape? Who knows IF it will appear? It is exactly that- the uncertainty of Black People's future and the irrefutability of white people's past- that behooves intelligent Blacks to do the safe thing. In light of the prevalence of racial depreciation in the United States, is it safe for Black People to put the destiny of Black People at the mercy of a white power decision?

The Jews of Weimar Germany did not do the safe thing. Max Liebermann, a Jewish painter, made the following statement: "Like a horrible nightmare the abrogation [nullification] of equal rights [in Germany] weighs upon us all, but especially upon those Jews who, like me, had surrendered themselves to the dream of assimilation..." [as quoted by Brenner.] Why did he surrender himself to "the dream of assimilation?" Because his intellectual flaws and self rejection rendered him incapable of making a common sense decision.

Georg Hermann, a famous Jewish writer, lamented the following. "We experience a great disappointment with the Germans and we still experience it today, every hour. Let me say openly a harsh word, why conceal it or hush up?! The Germans proved to be bad keepers of the seal of humanity." [as quoted by Brenner.]

Georg Hermann was deported to a death camp. Even at that moment of finality, his intellectual flaws emerged; else he would not have considered his criticism of the Germans "a harsh word." His words were not harsh, but they were real. The Germans, and white power in general, do not consider "the seal of humanity" a high priority item.

Hermann's self rejection and denial of a common sense decision would not allow him to voluntarily face up to that reality. He was too smart to learn the easy way, so he was forced to learn the hard way.

Merely a common sense decision on the part of Black People would preclude any further consideration of that possibility. Unfortunately, too many African-Americans are incapable of making a common sense decision of that magnitude. Time will tell.

The American Vote: Black Friend Or Foe?

INTRODUCTION

"Yes, these old folks had a
dream book, but the pages
went blank and it failed to give
them the number." R. Ellison

Some people in the United States have an un-examined fear of not voting. This is particularly true within certain small sectors of the African-American community. Let Us briefly examine the vote and try to determine if there is a substantial basis for the attachment so many Black individuals have to it. But first, some recurring figures.

In 1994, approximately 75 million people voted in the national elections. In 1996 the figure was approximately 96 million. If we allow that there are approximately 75 million individuals who are not old enough to vote, that will mean that approximately 120 million voting-aged individuals did not vote in 1994 and approximately 100 million did not vote in 1996. Thus, out of the two most recent national elections in the United States, the number of voting-aged individuals who did not vote was greater than that of those who actually voted. Clearly, a huge number of individuals in this country do not think voting is the powerful instrument it is professed to be.

Take note! The number of voting-aged white individuals who did not vote in either the 1994 or 1996 national elections is greater than the entire Black population of this country. What this means is that democracy, white power style, maintains a reserve supply of voters in much the same way capitalism maintains a reserve supply of laborers. Just as the reserve labor supply protects the interests of big business, the reserve voting supply protects the interests of the political status quo. To wit, if all of the whites who voted in the 1994 or 1996 national elections were to drop dead, and every Black person in this country decided to vote as a block for certain candidates and/or issues, the white power system could still effectively neutralize the Black vote by mobilizing less than 40% of the individuals who had failed to vote in either of the two most recent national elections. In the light of such an overwhelming imbalance, several questions emerge. Let's review some of them.

QUESTIONS ABOUT VOTING

Question #1. Will not voting hurt Black People in the United States of America?

Voting, in and of itself, is not capable of benefiting or hurting anyone. White America's founding fathers designed America's political structure that way. Because of their fear of "people power," America's founding fathers made sure the vote would be a weak, almost negligible element in the political process. They made voting a passive activity, and power politics is hardly impacted on by passive activities. They also made certain that voters would not have the constitutional authority to force their elected officials to follow the mandate of the voters. And, America's founding fathers made certain that voters would not have the constitutional authority to enact or enforce laws.

Additionally, voters vote based on promises made by a candidate. What a candidate promises and what he or she attempts to deliver as an elected official don't necessarily have anything to do with one another. We are all familiar with that reality. We are just as familiar with the fact that the vote of the people carries less weight than the vote of special electoral bodies. Even white American historians admit that Rutherford B. Hayes received fewer popular votes than his opponent in 1876, but Hayes became president. And, as soon as present-day white historians can separate themselves from the mirage of lies that masquerade as current American history, they will admit that John F. Kennedy's victory over Richard Nixon is clouded as well.

The electoral process (voting) is designed to play a very minor role in white power's political process. The political process, the power game, the activities that define and construct America's reality, are far removed from the voting arena. The political process is an inside job, an "in-house" continuum that revolves around branch dynamics; lobbying efforts, legislative processes, executive processes, judicial processes, etc. The everyday voter has practically zero influence on this political continuum.

There is little doubt: If Black People did not vote there would probably be fewer Black congress persons, fewer minority businesses receiving government contracts, fewer Black students attending white colleges and universities, fewer Black professors teaching at white colleges and universities, fewer successful Blacks in the mainstream entertainment, fewer Black media people receiving advertising monies from white America, etc. In short, there would be fewer Black individuals who seem to experience the white American dream. But would that mean Black People as a whole would be worse off? Not at all. As residents of the United States, We would be at least equal to Our present condition of less than first class citizens. As more likely contributors to an independent Black reality, We would not only be on the road to completeness, We would immediately begin to experience and feel the power of that completeness.

Many individuals do not understand how white

power functions. My understanding of white America has convinced me that "progress" and socially responsible legislation (like civil rights, voting rights, equal employment bills, etc.) are not a consequence of the power or threat of the Black vote. Even as We were shackled by Jim Crow in the 1870s and 1880s, We continued to forge ahead, recognized how to satisfy Our needs and maintained relative cohesion as a race of people. Yet, even as We freely voted in the 1980s and 1990s, We not only lost political and financial ground in the white arena, We found Ourselves farther and farther removed from ANY center of power. For Us, voting produced little (if anything at all).

Early civil rights legislation was passed on the tail of the War Between the States, not to bring equality to Black People but to control the political clout of southern whites. Likewise, the civil rights legislation of the 1960s was not intended to help Black People, its was intended to keep Black People from destroying white power's property and overwhelming white power's correctional system. None of this legislation had much of anything to do with "the vote," particularly the Black vote.

The most effective "voting" Black People did was in the 1860s (when Blacks walked off the plantations and stopped being slaves) and the 1950s and 1960s (when businesses were boycotted and property was destroyed on a grand scale). When We "vote" like that, white America's political process goes into high gear in order to placate Us until We cool off. But We should not want to remain in a system that requires Us to vote like that before We can get anything worthwhile accomplished. Even then, the white power system simply placates Us until We cool off, undoes as many of its lollipop changes as quickly as possible thereafter, and continues with anti-Black Power business as usual.

We should not want to remain in a position where We have to repeatedly spin Our tires in the same mud hole or fight the same old ineffective battles over and over and over again.

Question #2. Is there, in fact, the real likelihood that Black People can wield power by voting in America's elections?

In a word, "No!" White America's political process is not designed to accommodate Black Power. America's political process will absorb some individuals of color, provided that those individuals have demonstrated their safety-- their allegiance to white power and their scorn or distrust of Black Power. But Black individuals (and any other individuals of color) who have been absorbed by white power institutions will not be of much benefit to the Black masses. That is why the steady and continual decrease in the percentage of the population that is actually white is not that indicative of an impending shift in the essence of white America. Even when they have been a numerical minority, white people have managed to be dominant. Why? Because they have focused on institutionalizing a white power system and convincing non-whites to support that system. It is their system that projects the myths that prevail and dominate. Even if the primary functionaries and operatives are non-white, their white system carries on and retains the essence of whiteness.

I might add, as something of an aside, that the assertion that the Black vote is important because it can "swing" certain elections in favor of one or the other party is totally unfounded. The swing vote in this country belongs to white democrats and white independents who have a tendency to vote republican whenever they feel the need to do so. A simple look at the numbers will reveal that, theoretically, a republican should never win a national election in this country, but republicans win nearly as regularly as democrats. How is this possible? It is possible because white non-republicans regularly vote for republican candidates. It is this vote, which is quite substantial, not the relatively minor Black vote, that "swings" elections and generates otherwise improbable outcomes.

#3. Does it really matter that much if Black individuals vote for the candidates or issues of their choice?

Yes it does. To vote is to support a candidate or an issue, but more profoundly, it is to accept the legitimacy of the system. To cast your vote for the candidate of your choice in white America's elections is to also voice your support of the white power system. It is to say that the system deserves to be supported in spite of its negative qualities, that the damaging effects of racism are outweighed by the benefits the system provides, that the overall harm done to human beings is less of a factor than the overall good that the system delivers. By voting or not voting, We tell the Black and white people of America that developments in this country are either satisfactory or unsatisfactory, and We deliver the same message to people throughout the world. I wrote about this several years ago. The following is an edited paraphrase of that article:

> It's an election year, 1976. It is a time when people in America cast ballots on questions that are strictly American. It is a time when a people participates in a political process which recognizes that all of them are of the same family, are of the same nation and have common problems.

PLAYING BLACK CHEAP

It is a time when a people chooses one of several candidates because that candidate is representative of a frame of mind that will attempt to eliminate the common problems that afflict the "common people." The "common people" in America are all white and their common problem is getting a labor force that will support their economy and allow them to live a life of ease and comfort. Until this problem is solved, they will elect new representatives every two, four or six years because that is what the vehicle white people structured (the constitution) calls for.

Black People in the United States of America are not part of the "common people." The common people conduct themselves according to a general outline called the constitution, but other people are not allowed to do so. Special rules have to be developed for other people, rules that guarantee them special rights like "civil rights" and "voting rights," and special concessions like "affirmative action" and "set-asides." These rights and concessions are special because they are temporary and conditional. They might be taken away at any time because they apply to residents who are not generally accepted as part of the "common people."

However, Black People do play a role in America's "common problem." As a matter of fact, from the point of view of many of the "common people," Black People are a large part of the "common problem." The common people can't live in ease and comfort to the degree they want to because Black People refuse to willingly provide the land and labor that could elevate whites to Easy Street. What's more, Blacks insist on clamoring about things such as justice, equality, socialism and humanity. This produces slight disorders among the common people (like increased poverty, police brutality against whites, astronomical food and insurance costs, etc.) because whites have to sacrifice some of their goodies and give them to the Blacks and other minorities. However, the common people realize that these disorders are not fundamental. They will disappear as soon as the "common problem" is solved.

The experts among the common people have determined that the common problem can be solved in either of two ways. It can be solved by physically eliminating those special people who refuse to be passive and work for the good of the common people or it can be solved by forcing all special people to surrender their land and labor into the hands of the common people. But who among the common people can make either choice a reality? There is no unanimous response, so the common people go to the polls to determine who the majority of them feels can get the job done.

Special people can voice their opinion (vote) on the issue also. The common people agreed to allow this with the provision that special people stick strictly to the issues and candidates (special people can't make any extraneous or unsolicited suggestions). Those who are unwilling to stick to the issues and candidates as laid out by the common people need not vote because the vote does not recognize the validity of anything else.

What does this mean to Black People in the United States? It means the following: We have the choice of voting or not voting, but which should it be? If We vote We might elect an individual who sympathizes with Our "safe" aspirations, someone who might attempt to improve the lot of some Black individuals and protect Us or "empower" some of Us within a white power context. But when We vote We simultaneously admit that Black People should either leave the country or submit Our labor and land (Africa, Caribbean, North America, etc.) to white people and their white power system. By voting, We also admit that the question the common people seek to resolve is a valid question; that some people have to be enslaved or unjustifiably exploited so that others might live comfortably. And, when We vote We de-prioritize Our Blackness and question the need for its existence. As such, We help to establish a single American people that is based solely on what is white, and We disregard everything else.

People all over the known world are watching Black People in the United States. People all over the world realize that to vote is to admit the legitimacy of the issue. Therefore, We must be careful about the images and impressions We send them. What impression of America would people throughout the world have if Black People refused, as a matter of policy, to participate in America's electoral process? What impression of America would people all over the world have if We consistently made public Our dissatisfaction with the white power system? What impression of America would people of the world have if We consistently publicized the pernicious and anti-human underpinnings of the white power system? What impression of America would people throughout the world have if We made it crystal clear that the hidden destructiveness of white power politics and economics far outweigh their apparent rewards? Would the Chinese people be in favor of converting to this type of system if they knew what

Black People know? Would Cuban citizens be so eager to defect to this country if they knew what We know? Would the people of Russia have supported Boris Yeltsin and the conversion to capitalism if they had known as much about capitalism as We know? Probably not. In that light, it is clear that, by voting in white America's elections, Black People in this country play a major role in the advancement of the white power system throughout the world. When We vote, We are telling the people of the world that the white power system, though faulty, is all right for the most part. What a misleading message that is!

The essential question facing Us should not revolve around whether or not We should vote, but how to genuinely empower Black People, help Us overcome the aura of voting and seek to build an independent set of parameters for Our people. If Black People do not vote in white America's elections, can the political process be used against Us more easily? Of course it can. But the reality remains: the political process can be used, has been used and will continue to be used against Us whether We vote or not.

The vote, for Black People, is like an enticing carrot. It swings before Our eyes and mind, suggesting sooo very much. But it turns out to be a carrot that, even if eaten, has no nutritional value. It can be chewed and swallowed, and it will fill a stomach up; but it doesn't help to rebuild the cells, restore energy, reenforce the immune system or revitalize one's creative essence. As a matter of fact, it fights against these essential functions. Is that a carrot worth investing in or relying on? I think not.

POTENTIAL ADVANTAGES OF NOT VOTING

Instead of concentrating on the potential harm not voting might cause, let's take a look at the potential good not voting can generate.

(1) Since necessity is one of the mothers of invention, if Black People boycotted voting altogether, a whole new world of possibilities would have to open up to Us. By rejecting the only form of "government" that We are consciously aware of and accustomed to, We would be forced to imagine and explore alternative political parameters. We would learn that many former African-Americans are claiming citizenship with the Black Washitaw Nation and are already governing themselves, right here on land that an uninformed person would think belongs to the United States! We would also pay more attention to the activities of independence seekers and Black nationalists, and not only learn more about governments like the Republic of New Afrika, but take them more seriously.

In short, We would find out that some individuals, Black and non-Black, are already discussing alternatives and making strides that would give Us more control than We could ever experience as "citizens" of the United States. We need to know about these things, and not voting would force Us to learn about them.

(2) Not voting would force Us to take on responsibilities that mature adults normally take on. We would learn, for example, that We can not only take on these responsibilities, We can do a better job of producing the results We desire than the United States government. We would learn that We CAN establish and finance independent, Black educational institutions, that We CAN educate Ourselves more thoroughly than the

United States government, and that We CAN produce more productive and well-developed Black individuals than the United States government. We would discover that We CAN shelter and clothe Black People, We CAN establish construction companies and build houses just as well as anybody else, and We CAN establish manufacturing businesses that produce all of the clothing Our people need. We would also learn that We CAN feed Our people. We don't have to rely on outsiders, should not rely on outsiders, to perform those vital functions. The only reason We presently do so is because the United States government has bullied and seduced Us into turning to white power to serve Our needs. White power will never adequately serve the needs of Black People, and if We stopped voting in the United States elections, We would not only realize that, We would be forced to act in accordance with that realization.

We, Black People, can police Ourselves better than any of the jurisdictions that comprise the United States of America. We can establish the appropriate institutions and agencies and carry out the myriad of functions that policing requires, and We could do it in a manner that will benefit Our communities and help Us grow as a people. We are also capable of establishing a national defense system, establishing the necessary international contacts and implementing Our own foreign affairs agenda, formulating economic policies and financial principles that will be good for Our people and carrying out all of the other functions that all independent people carry out. All We need to do, as a first step, is become politically mature and brave enough to accept the immediate financial "downside" of not voting. After taking that first step, We will be in a position to make huge strides toward the political and economic "upside" of not voting.

Of all the non-white races in the United States of

America, white America fears Black People the most. As a matter of fact, white power America fears Black People more than it fears the USSR, China or Cuba. Why? Not only because We have demonstrated that We can bring white America to its knees, but because Our contributions to white power give it a degree of substance and sustainability that it would not otherwise possess. If Black People refused to continue making those contributions to white power, white power would be reduced to only a shadow of itself. If We make contributions to a Black Power structure instead, if We contributed Our energy, genius and wealth to a Black Power structure instead of a white power structure, We could make Black Power an international reality that would drastically upset and change power relationships throughout the world. White power functionaries know this, and it scares them to death.

We haven't convinced Ourselves of Our power yet, but We have definitely convinced white America. If We got rid of Our misguided attachment to the United States vote, We would learn what white America already knows.

(3) By not voting, We would learn that We can do well for Ourselves outside of the white power context. African-Americans do not realize how much their perspectives are tied to a white power context. African-Americans have been made so narrow minded that they default see and interpret everything from a white power perspective (what is good for "the country"). Certainly, it is done without full awareness, but it is done nonetheless. By a force of hand, African-Americans would learn that they can relate to the world's peoples, governments and organizations in a much healthier fashion, and be granted much more power and respect than white America is willing to grant.

(4) By not voting as a matter of policy, Black People would also rid Ourselves of fake white liberals and make it clear to the world that Black People do not agree with white power principles and machinations. Those whites who are really concerned about justice and liberty will realize that Black Power is not a threat to the average white person and maintain a righteous course, while the rest of them, most of them I might add, will come to the realization that they cannot control the Black struggle and immediately or gradually abandon their "liberalism." We need to make it clear that We can steer Our struggle in the direction that best suits the interests of Black People. We will have a lot easier time doing that if We don't have to overcome the resistance of white "liberals" who insist on mapping out the course of action and having their hands on the steering wheel.

(5) By abandoning the United States vote, Black People would be able to represent Our interests with greater clarity and efficiency. Within the white power context, a Black individual who represents genuine Black Power would have to revolve his or her platform around the transformation of the white power system. It is silly for Us to think that We can transform this system by voting in elections, and it is wasteful for Us to spend even the tiniest amount of Our time and energy trying to do so (saving white power's system is not Black People's responsibility!). If We stop voting, We can devote more time and energy to building a system that will serve Us well and stop trying to transform a system that is hopelessly rotten to the core.

We pay a huge price for participating in white America's voting process, a price that we are not fully aware of. If We refuse to vote, We would pay a smaller price, get greater long term benefits and, just as importantly, become somewhat aware of Our potential as an independent people. Self-determination, control of Our own destiny, independence from an anti-Black and anti-human white power system; that's a lot to give up for a vote!

And when one adds the fact that it is a hypocritical vote, a powerless vote, a vote clouded in Reconstruction-like mysticism, it goes beyond being a mere sacrifice, it becomes self-mutilating and self-destructive.

CONCLUSION

Within the present scheme of things, the United States vote, like a lollipop, is there for the licking. Black People keep licking it and licking it because it somehow appeals to Us, but the fact of the matter is that it is destroying Our taste buds, rotting Our teeth, attacking Our digestive enzymes and ruining Our appetite for valuable political nourishment. Not licking that lollipop could eliminate a serious threat to Our community, Our health and Our well-being, and propel Us into an entirely different set of power parameters.

Thus, the failure to vote could be good for Black People in the United States of America. Since white America's electoral process is not an empowering process, the failure to vote, in and of itself, can not harm Us. The weak of heart might claim that if Black People fail to vote, "the system" could justify its failure to respond to Our concerns, but such talk isn't worthy of a serious Black person's time and attention. The fact of the matter is that there is nothing, NOTHING, about voting in United States elections that can eliminate the ability of the white power system to abuse Black People in America. The weak among Us, who also are, unfortunately, the most "successful," will never be able to accept the truth of that statement. That partly explains why they cannot see beyond the vote, and why We, as a People, are content riding as passengers in white people's "car."

Take heed! As long as We follow the lead of inept Black individuals, and as long as We fear the consequences of breaking with traditional approaches to Our liberation, We will continue to NOT experience self-realization, We will continue to NOT experience political independence and We will continue to NOT prove to Ourselves that We can make it quite well using Our own genius, Our own talents, Our own know-how and Our own institutions. We must not allow the fear that controls a few of Us handicap all of Us. Yes, there is that fear, that fear that mentally disables certain Black individuals and handcuffs them to white America's vote. That fear is that, if Black People don't vote, white people will enact legislation that is specifically designed to harm Black People and hinder Our development. Such a fear is a warped person's admission that white people despise Us, view Us with contempt and will use every available opportunity to cripple Us. Yet, the very same mentally disabled Black individuals who fear white America's malicious instincts toward Black People urge Black People to make sacrifice after sacrifice for the sake of "integrating" with white people, accepting white people's status as the dominant group and accepting Our role as a dependent, "dark white" minority. That is a prime example of warped thinking. That is a prime example of the type of thinking that will keep Black People at the mercy of white people and white power forever.

The vote??? That is not the issue. The issue is Our reality as a mature and equal People. The issue is Our right and need to govern Ourselves. The issue is the establishment of an independent Black nation. When We recognize any issue short of that, We play Black People cheap. We have played Black People cheap for too long and too often already.

To see this flag in color and order it go online to: http://
asetbooks.com/Us/Mall/Blackidentityitems.html

EUROPE: WHITE AMERICA'S ROOTS!

Should Black People Really Want To Integrate With White People?

INTRODUCTION

Europe is one of the areas of the world that early Black People migrated to and explored. Some Blacks, for whatever reasons, remained in Europe and experienced physical, psychological, spiritual and ideological changes that resulted in the existence of a non-Black race of people. In the modern world, these descendants of the original inhabitants of Europe are called white people and/or Caucasians. These people multiplied and took on group character traits unique to themselves, and Europe became the continent that is generally recognized as their homeland.

Europe is the land mass that contains several groups of white people, but historically they have been unable to get along with each other. Just as the European family is a unit that separates and facilitates division within European communities, European nations evolved in a way that enabled white "elites" to easily exploit the divisive elements found within and among the various white tribes.

During modern times three of the countries that have kept themselves at the center of this European schism are England, France and Germany. The other countries have played important roles as well from time to time, and Russia has recently emerged as a major player. We are going to explore many of these countries and get a basic understanding of what each meant and continues to mean to the establishment and maintenance of white power.

There is a constant thread running throughout the European countries and people, particularly western Europeans. That constant thread is the drive to conquer, to "prove' something, to dominate; and because of that the history of Europe has been characterized by barbarism, greed, warfare and snobbishness. Until the 20th century, petty quarrels and ethnocentric prejudices controlled the internal affairs of Europe, so much so that in order to understand Europe, one must understand the concepts of western Europeans and eastern Europeans.

It is true. In very real ways, Europe is more than one continent. To wit, there is western Europe and there is eastern Europe. The conflicts, both material and cultural, run rampant and deep, promote divisions (a reality that conflicts vividly with the white unity images white power leaders promote) and keep white power vulnerable. This deep basis for division is crucial to an understanding not only of white power, but of the myth of white power.

Yes, We will come to understand France (The Sly, Restrained Fox), Great Britain/England (The Weak Wolf), Germany (The Strong Wolf) and Russia (The Still Unrefined Wolf). And We will come to understand the third element of the European mix, the Papacy and its Pope. We will see how the kings of Europe have ripped off the people in the name of political legitimacy in much the same way as the Pope, who has done so in the name of religious mythology. The Pope goes on, even though weakened by competition from other religions, while the kings have been replaced by the state, constitutions, governments, presidents, etc; each shamelessly insisting on its right to rule, its "legitimacy." And the European people go on being screwed because they are poorly organized, because they give allegiance to an ideology that is designed to abuse them, because they are suckers for a lie well told, and because too many of them have been rendered either incapable of taking control of their own destiny, or too irresponsible to do so.

In this essay We will come to understand white people-- in the United States and abroad— and be able to determine if Black People should want to integrate with them. They are very capable, they should not be taken lightly and they presently dominate world affairs. But, more than anything else, they have the habit of acting despicably--- and no white history book can hide that reality.

FRANCE

The countries of Europe, the bases of operation of different branches of white power, can be compared to a den of malcontents. This is not to suggest that all Europeans, all white individuals, are maladjusted, it merely recognizes that their totality is disproportionately dominated by activities and processes that well-developed people frown upon. That is not an anti-white or prejudicial statement, it is a statement of fact, and We must address it as such.

Among the major white countries in Europe one finds England/Great Britain (which closely resembles a weak wolf), Germany (a strong wolf), Russia (an unrefined wolf) and France (a sly, restrained fox). With the exception of Russia, We could cover these countries in either order. For no particular reason, I will begin with France.

French leadership was responsible for the first official union of the European church and state. Charlemagne, whose roots were Franco-Germanic and whose empire covered much of present day Germany and France, is responsible for this accomplishment. Thus, it was the French elite who officially united the religious ideology of the Catholic Church with the political ideology of white power, an unholy alliance that has helped white people from Europe terrorize each other and other people of the world for more than 1200 years. This unholy alliance is a cornerstone of white world domination, and Europeans appreciate the French for having made this alliance a reality.

But France's "religious" contribution to European development and the spread of white power does not stop there. It was the French who, on the tail of the 12th century, stopped the spread of Islam into Western Europe. The Islamic armies of Turkey had overwhelmed most of the other European tribes and countries, and the Europeans had resigned themselves, for the most part, to converting to Islam. But the French, more inept than most major western European warriors, somehow repulsed the Turks and started a Christian counter-offensive. By way of this major military accomplishment (around 1200 AD), France saved European Christianity. Without that victory, much of Western Europe would likely be Islamic today, and the conflict between eastern whites (non-European) and western whites would probably be manifesting itself in different ways.

The French people have historically voiced more support for the rights of the common person than the other western European people. Notice: I said the French people, not the French government or the French elites. The individual's life, the individual's liberty and the individual's right to pursue happiness have traditionally meant more to the French than the English, German, Spanish, etc. Most of the grand moments in European history that championed the rights of the common person either took place in France or were inspired by the activities of the French masses. Most notable are the French Revolutions of 1787 and 1848. As a matter of fact, if one omits those two revolutions and the Bolshevik Revolution (1917 in Russia), there is no other European "revolution" of any duration worth mentioning. Most of the other "revolutions" that European educators refer to were actually efforts of one elite group to overthrow another elite group. As such, they were not revolutions at all; they were coup d'états, political acts that overthrew one elitist centered government and replaced it with another elitist centered government.

Thus, France, in many ways, has been the hub of Western Europe's revolutionary activity. But as strong as the French people's commitment is to the rights of the individual, it must be understood that they cherish this belief within the context of white power, not human equality. That represents a fundamental contradiction between white people who champion life, liberty and the pursuit of happiness and Black People who champion the same causes.

When Columbus tripped over the Americas, the French took a different approach to exploration than the Spanish, Portuguese and English. France established colonies in different parts of the world, but their concept of an empire was affected by a less coarse greed than that of their cruder sisters and brothers. In spite of this, the French elite prospered and managed to keep themselves in the forefront of European developments, often assuming the influence of a major world power. But the French elite made serious mistakes between 1785 and 1815, and those mistakes turned France into a perpetual also-ran, militarily speaking. Not long after, France began to take on different modes of operation. The French elite, realizing that France's days as a world power were over, began transforming France into the sly, restrained fox that it is today.

France's romantic attachment to the little person and its competition with the English elites makes it easy to understand why France contributed so much to the birth and development of Europe's grand baby, the United States of America. The French elite helped finance the American Revolution when others shied away, and the French people envisioned America as a new hope for the common person's cause. Unfortunately, the French people's concern for the common person was too weak to penetrate the instincts of the French elite, and too under- promoted and financed to cross national boundaries or impact on the priorities of other major European countries. This concern took root in America, however, but it was a feeble root. The roots implanted by the Germans and the English (to be discussed later) were much more intense, much more appealing and much more representative of the gut instincts of Europe's stepchildren in the United States. In America, the rights of the common person were frequently debated and talked about by America's emerging elite, but America's legal structure never seriously considered authenticating and empowering the common person. As America grew and her elite became more aware of America's options and potential, America resorted to what she felt most comfortable with-- the aggressive, militaristic European mode of conduct, characterized by coarse instincts and reactions, not civilized responses, processes and applications. In America the revolutionary and "equality" penchant of the French masses were romanticized, bombasted, rhapsodized--- and after all was said and done, rendered impotent.

But what explains the unusual concern of the French for the common person? It is clear that at some point the consciousness of the French diverged slightly from that of other major Europeans, and it was prior to the earlier mentioned realization that took place after 1815. The initial divergence probably has its roots in the early periods of European tribalism, long before the so-called Dark Ages. During that period, as now, the European tribes constantly warred with each other. The French, being some of the least capable warriors, were regularly dominated and humiliated on the battlefield. Centuries before the time of Julius Caesar, it was well known that (1) French soldiers would panic and run in the midst of battle and (2) French women would bare their breasts and be ready to accommodate the invading soldiers after the French men had succumbed to defeat. It is not unlikely, then, that the French people experienced a feeling of collective deficiency or inadequacy. To cope with that feeling and placate their collective ego, they could have collectively compensated, psychologically speaking, by toning down their superiority complexes and coarse impulses and emphasizing other avenues to gaining completeness.

Present day France was set in stone by two huge processes that took place simultaneously between 1785 and 1815. First, the French people proved to be incapable of relying on their own energy, so the French Revolution stalled. This began a constant waning of France's preoccupation with the rights of the common person. Secondly, the French elite lost control of San Domingo, the richest colony in the world. By the end of the San Domingo Revolution, the French elite had not only lost its riches, but its powerful army as well. The Blacks of San Domingo devastated the French military. As a result, Napoleon Bonaparte gave up all hope of supporting the empire the French had established in America and practically gifted the Louisiana Territory to the United States. France's days as a world power had come to an end, even as the Napoleonic Wars raged and France and Great Britain waged war for supremacy against one another. But those wars meant nothing; they were contests between has-beens. By 1816, France's sun had definitely set and Great Britain's was descending rapidly.

As concern for the common person waned and the French military weakened, the French elite searched for new sources of riches. France watched capitalism step forward and the Industrial Revolution mold new economic realities, and the French elite, like their European brethren, realized that salvation resided in Africa, the Black continent, the militarily weak continent. And it was there that the countries of Western Europe converged and stole the riches white people needed to take them through the 20th century and beyond. With the proper amount of blood-letting and theft, the French became richer than ever (although less militarily imposing), and more convinced that their salvation was inextricably tied into the politics and dominance of white power. The French, like the other Europeans, rededicated themselves to promoting and maintaining white power no matter what it took.

Great Britain/England: The Weak Wolf

England, the "mother country" of the United States of America.

Due to prevailing propaganda, when one thinks of the French, the rights of the common man, within a European context, come to mind. When one thinks of the Germans, crude aggressiveness and efficiency, within a European context, come to mind. When one thinks of England, the "mother country" of the United States of America, the image of hooliganism and all of its erosive by-products gnaws steadily into one's mind. As much as white people are alike, whether in France, Germany or any other part of the world, the English are the ones that stand out when one thinks of hoodlums, street gang mentalities, lack of decorum, baseness and red neck intolerance. The English are the perennial losers who set their sights on America, passed on their genetic code to the American colonies, and burdened the United States with powerfully anti-social inclinations. Without the English influence, the United States could not have created a wild, wild, west. Unfortunately, the English influence is more American than any other, and that says volumes about the inability of "Americans" to act civilly and play a progressive role in the international arena.

How could a people fail to develop as completely as did the English? I can't say I know for sure. If we go back 2000 years, we see European powers that were not highly organized, socially speaking. As a result, they kept only a few reliable records. Much of what is known about the early French and Germans comes from records maintained by powers like Greece and Rome. Unlike France and Germany, however, England is not connected to the rest of the European continent. England is an island, and the water that separated it from the rest of Europe also enabled it to unfold in relative obscurity. Let's take a look at what probably happened.

Before the time of Christ, no one knew the size of the English island. In fact, before the time of Julius Caesar, talk of the English people was as much fantasy as reality. So little was actually known about the English that some scholars suggested that England was a name for a land that did not exist.

But England did exist. At around 800 BC, some Celts invaded Britain and established a tribal structure. As many as 100 kings would rule at the same time. The Celts constantly fought among themselves for inheritance rights, land and power. When they were not fighting each other, they were attacking others, incurring huge debts and draining money from local provinces in order to pay them off. Women were inferior and insignificant; one Celtic woman could be the shared property of a dozen Celtic men. Of primary concern, however, was the maintenance of a balance of power throughout the tribes. Therefore, Celtic laws of succession dictated that kings divide their land amongst their sons in order to keep huge kingdoms from persisting. A huge kingdom that spanned generations was too threatening to their way of life.

Julius Caesar set his sights on the English island because he had heard rumors of England's riches. When he arrived (around 57 BC), he found the Britons armed and waiting. English tribes had heard he was coming and united to fight him. Caesar defeated them easily (the English, in spite of their empire building, have a history of military inefficiency), but found no riches and very little else of interest. Still, Caesar made Britain a part of the Roman Empire.

A decade later, under Emperor Claudius, the romanizing of Britain began. Claudius established a system of roads and made use of England's excellent artisans and cloth makers. 200 years later, Constantine made Christianity the official religion of Rome and, by extension, England. Prior to then, a powerful but questionable priesthood had controlled England's religious and educational activities.

Being part of the Roman Empire brought England into constant contact with the rest of the European world. With the collapse of the Roman Empire two centuries after Constantine, there was a collapse of social order in England. This condition continued for over a century, followed by a settling down period and the emergence of several strong kingdoms.

By the year 600, non-Celtic whites like the Angles and Saxons had taken over. During this period, seven kingdoms dominated Britain. In the late 600s, the Archbishop of Canterbury set up a centralized system of bishops and introduced a new concept of kingship and church government. Surprisingly, this proved to be the first step in a nearly 800-year process toward English nationalism and developing the English state. Sometime during the first 250 to 300 years of this process, Hamlet's Danes and the Vikings of Norway managed to move in, dominate and divide England between them; the Danes taking the north (including Scotland and Ireland) and the Vikings taking the south, which included present-day London. The Viking kings required all citizens of wealth to join the military arm of their royal family. The Danes in Viking controlled areas rebelled and were brutally crushed. Later, the Vikings invaded the Danes in the north. The old tribal and clan systems were replaced by a feudal system that required each man to have a lord that was legally responsible for him. No national law existed, and local customs prevailed that were enforced by representatives of the king. Not surprisingly, conflict between the feudal lords and kingly authority was frequent.

So, up until around the year 1000, England can be summed up as follows: (1) its early inhabitants were lowly organized Celts; (2) the Celts were violent people but inefficient warriors; (3) the Celts, astute artisans and cloth makers, were administratively, financially and militarily dominated by several invaders; (4) a centralized system of bishops was installed that enhanced the church's claim to the right to govern and emboldened an emerging elite and (5) neither the church, king or elite respected the human rights of the common person.

Since the year 1000, the history of England has been characterized by battles between the church, royalty and elites, battles among royal relatives over land, power and succession, and battles between royal families and elites from other countries; all for the right to control the minds and wealth of the common people.

The English connection between kings and religion rested on the proposition that whatever would generate an advantage was worth promoting as the gospel. When the church felt it had the upper hand, it claimed it had the right to govern and tried to weaken the authority of the king. When the king felt he had the upper hand, he claimed he had the right to govern and threatened to use his military to squash the church. When the church felt weak, it would attempt to ally with a king and grant that king "divine" protection. And, when the king felt the need to do so, he would claim that he was a direct descendant of God and try to force the church to validate his claims.

Thus, we see the battles between the church and king over the sovereignty of Scotland in 1284. We see, in 1519, Henry 8 losing his bid to become Holy Roman Emperor, breaking with the Pope and establishing the Church of England as a result. And we see Charles I claiming that he was divine and causing the English Civil War in 1642. The ultimate victim in each of these battles, and many others of similar ilk, was not the church or the king, but the common people.

The victims in the other battles were also the common people. In 1350, Wat Tyler led a rebellion of the common people against royal abuse. The royalty was so militarily inept that Wat and his men succeeded in capturing the king and intimidating his court. But instead of killing the king and trying to establish a just government, Wat and his men negotiated with the king and, taking him at his word that he would implement agreed upon changes, returned to their separate farms. As soon as they separated, the king had them murdered one by one.

In 1603, James VI became king and established the Protestant Church in Scotland. In 1689, the friction between elite-minded persons and the royalty led to a Bill of Rights that legally established the relationship between the king and a parliamentary form of government, and began a movement away from royal-kingly rule. The post of Prime Minister came into being (1721) as a result of this friction, and the king became a figurehead. From that time on, the battle for control of the common person in England was between the church, the new elite and the government/state. The king, like the common person, had become negligible.

Not long after Columbus tripped over America, the elites from England competed with the elites from other European countries for America's riches. Because of England's artisans and cloth makers, England's economy had long revolved around trade as much as agriculture. So, the concept of an exchange medium had been toyed with, and English businessmen and government leaders had recognized the value of implementing diverse business principles, including allowing the workers more freedom than was the norm in Europe. In fact, as early as the 1200s, seeds of capitalism had sprouted in England. All of these gave the English a head start in what was to become a factory dominated industrialized world.

This head start is mainly responsible for the establishment of the British Empire, which expanded not because of the strength of the English but the military weakness of North America, Asia, Australia and Africa. It began in North America in the 1600s, but by 1780 the American colonies were already lost. In 1801, the English king relinquished his claim to France and the British Empire faded into a spider web collection of "commonwealths."

The English lack the smarts and efficiency that characterize the Germans, but they are every bit as determined. They are the typical bully type; relying on brute force, intimidation and underhandedness when they encounter the militarily weak, and proving themselves totally inept when they encounter an equal. But they are too coarse to allow their shortcomings to keep them from trying. They are too obtuse to realize when they should not attempt to do something, so they try and sometimes succeed.

What the British and other Caucasians are trying to do today is maintain white world power. Since World War II, the British have regarded the United States, their offspring, as the most capable guardian of white power. By being the United States' sidekick, the British can stick their chest out, hide behind the latest white bully and enjoy the benefits that white power has traditionally accorded them.

GERMANY

The German nation is barely 130 years old, being formally established in 1871. The history of the Germanic tribes, however, goes back much farther, and it is clear that the coarse, ancient roots, inclinations and tendencies prevail. As the Germanic tribes were more than 2000 years ago, so the German state is more than 2000 years later.

The terms Germanic and Gaul are at times almost interchangeable. In early times, this loose collection of anywhere from 250 to 275 tribes was nomadic to the core. They resisted settling down even after the benefits of an agricultural lifestyle were made known to them, preferring instead to hunt and live principally off of dead animals (meat) and milk products. Nutritionists now know that such a diet is one of the worst human beings can consume. Such a diet is not only bad for the physical development of people, but hinders their spiritual and social development as well. These developmental shortcomings jump out at the analytical person who takes a look at the German people and their general manner of conduct.

Among the early Germans (and all nomads), the military defense of the group was always the first concern. Therefore, all economic, moral and supernatural values were determined by principles of war. For instance: (1) it was only possible to enter the Germanic heaven (Valhalla) if you were killed on the field of battle; (2) it was considered lazy and cowardly to work for something if you could get it by killing or stealing from someone else; and (3) robbery was okay as long as it was outside the tribe. Their entire makeup revolved around aggressions, indiscretions, wars and more wars.

The early Germans knew only three gods; the sun, Vulcan and the moon. No goddess existed in their pantheon (religious hierarchy). However, German women relied on prophecies to determine when their men should go into battle. This reliance enabled Julius Caesar to break down their defenses and eventually defeat them when he conquered the world for Rome. Later the Germans adapted other people's gods to their pantheon. Not surprisingly, even the gods in Valhalla (heaven) spent their time fighting among themselves and getting drunk.

When the German leadership decided to desert an area, they would burn every one of their own villages in order to keep the weaker spirited families from deserting and staying behind; freedom of choice was not built into their habits and institutions. And, during war, the leaders were apt to set fire to any of their towns that could not be made impregnable. This mentality, this crude, one-sided, "my way or no way" mentality; one has to understand that in order to understand what

Germany is, what a German is.

But war, their efficiency at war, their love of war; that is what separated the Germans from their European brothers and sisters. Their thirst for war is what brought them fame, and their success at it helped brand the French and lace the English with shame. The German men waged devastating warfare, and their unpardonable sin was to flee during battle. They attacked not only people but everything that moved, including nature. They believed courage was attacking other people and taking their territories, and they spent practically all of their time in warlike pursuits and physical routines that hardened them against pain and fatigue. They were bigger than most Europeans, more vigorous trainers and more courageous fighters. All of this, combined with their reputation, red mustaches, fiery eyes and rugged demeanor, destroyed the will to fight of many of their white brothers and sisters.

To the Germans, war wounds were marks of honor. Along those lines, a young German male had the right to shave his beard only by moistening it with the blood of an enemy killed in battle. But it wasn't just war that distinguished the Germans. During his campaign against the Gauls, Julius Caesar noted that the Germans were an ingenious race who were very good at imitating and making use of other people's ideas. Julius Caesar was right. The Germans have long been an ingenious people, very capable of imitating others when it is to their advantage to do so. Thus, in addition to war, Germans have used smarts, efficiency and perseverance to get their way. "Whatever it takes" is what they come prepared to give. When Malcolm X spoke of "by any means necessary," almost any German would have intuitively understood what he was talking about.

More than 2000 years ago, such was the German

mentality, such were the German values, such were the German customs. More than 2000 years ago, such was what being a German was all about. More than 2000 years later, such is the German mentality, such are the German values, such are the German customs. More than 2000 years later, such is what being a German is all about.

But there is an important difference. Germany is not as obviously coarse as it was a couple thousand years ago. Today, Germany is pretty much like a refined wolf, albeit a crude degree of refinement. This evidenced itself with the recognition that the separate tribes needed to give up a bit of their individuality and unify for the sake of competing in a modern, European atmosphere of conflict. German university professors spoke of German nationalism and German artists and creative thinkers expressed German nationalism in their art and writings, but the person who was most influential in bringing this unification process to fruition was Otto von Bismarck.

Otto von Bismarck wanted German unity under the leadership and domination of Prussia. This became an established fact, for all intents and purposes, in 1871. After attaining that unity, Bismarck had to struggle with the Catholic Church, which was always in a dogfight with European governments over who would control the hearts, minds and pocketbooks of the European people. By way of the church's dogma of papal infallibility, it sought to extend the pope's "rights" and defend the church against encroachments made by the various European states.

Bismarck felt that words meant little or nothing; his method to unify Germany revolved around blood and iron. His blood and iron policy precipitated three wars and brought about the result Bismarck wanted.

But Bismarck was not a favorite of Kaiser Wilhelm, so the Kaiser dismissed Bismarck when he became king.

In the late 1870s, Kaiser Wilhelm, a medical blunder with typical German inclinations, entered Germany into the race for Africa. This mad rush by Europe for control of Africa resulted in World War I and the break-up of the German state. 15000 Blacks fought for Kaiser Wilhelm in World War I, but this fact had little impact on Adolf Hitler, who made the Blacks in Germany his first victims 20 years after the first war ended (even though they were tolerated for as long as they served a useful purpose). Hitler had Africans depicted as culturally primitive and used Germany's Department of Racial and Hereditary Welfare to sterilize many Blacks (removing the testicles of many young Black men) and kill even more. The German attitude toward Blacks was even clearer in the colony of Southwest Africa (Namibia), where 80% of the original inhabitants were killed and massacred so that a white colony could be established. I will not deal with it now, but it is important to note that Hitler blamed the Jews for bringing Blacks into Germany. For that he made the Jews pay.

More than 2000 years have come and gone, but the Germans essentially are as they have always been; lacking in the critical areas that characterize a civilized people. They, like the whites as a whole, are coarse, racist and ethnocentric, but the Germans are more efficient and warlike than their brothers and sisters. As world powers go, Germany is suited to play the role to the max, as it has historically done.

As has been the case historically, Germany will use its power, as whites are primed to do and have always done, to make war on other people and preserve the reign of white power and white world domination. Of that you can be sure.

RUSSIA

It is important to note that Russia is an eastern European country. All of the other principals discussed in this series are western European countries. The "elite" from western Europe have historically felt that eastern Europeans were coarse, backwards and lacking in development. Western European elites, then, have a superiority complex toward eastern Europeans (this explains the hoard of eastern European, particularly Polish, jokes). In all honesty, eastern Europeans have done little until recently to challenge the biases of their western brothers and sisters. That challenge has been spearheaded by Russia.

As late as the 800s AD, very little was known of Russia. Europeans as a rule recorded little of their development, and reliable information about Russia is harder to find than usual. According to what is available, some Slavic peoples occupied areas of eastern Europe for a while leading up to the 800s AD, when they were overcome by Scandinavian Vikings called Rus. These are probably the same type invaders that moved into France and England at or near the same time period. The founding of the first Russian dynasty, characterized by trade and cultural contact with Greece, has been traced to the latest stages of this period, the late 900s AD. Starting with the 900s and continuing for about 300 years, we can see many of the building blocks being laid that account for much of what Russia appears to be in the modern era.

[It will be important to note that Russia's outside influences were of Greek, not Roman, origins. Western Europeans, by contrast, used Rome as a developmental model. Thus, Russia took on habits, customs and an institutional demeanor that differed noticeably from those of its western siblings. These differences account for much of the lack of esteem western Europeans hold for eastern Europeans and are responsible for the economic, political and religious appearances that seem to distinguish the two. Close examination reveals that these apparent differences are simply different grades of fur on the same animal; different practices that represent the same corrosive and elitist approach to life.]

From the 900s on, Russia's development was characterized by the same type activities that characterized white people throughout Europe. There was consolidation and expansion, arguments and wars over succession when kings died (Russian customs recognized no line of descent), invasions and outside influences, conflicts between the king/royalty and the nobility, abuse of the common person (the peasants were made serfs) and clashes between the church and king over who had the right to drain the masses. Russia was intent on not adhering to the religion of the west. Russia adopted the Greek Orthodox religion, and when a union between the Greek Church and the Vatican (Pope) took place in 1439, Basil, Russia's king, not only failed to recognize it but put forces in motion that resulted in the establishment of a totally independent Russian Orthodox Church. Russia's elite recognized the importance of establishing ties with the west in other regards. Therefore, Russia began to officially introduce itself to western Europe's business and political community in the 1200s.

In 1462 the first great modern ruler of Russia emerged. He was Ivan III (the Great). In 1492, Ivan invaded Lithuania and made White and Red Russia part of his kingdom. Ivan also married into Greek royalty. This marriage was arranged by the Pope, who hoped to bring Russia under the umbrella of the Roman Catholic Church. The pope's scheme failed, but the contact introduced Russia's elite to different ideas about government and resulted in Ivan calling himself tzar (after Caesar).

In 1533, Russia's second great modern ruler took the throne. This was Ivan IV (the Terrible), who ruled until 1584. Ivan IV had himself crowned tzar (the first Russian king to formally do so), expanded the empire, gave trade rights to the British and formed other important links with the west.

Uncertainty about who had the right to succeed to the throne was a source of repeated warfare in Russia. In1613, a national assembly elected Michael Romanov tzar of Russia. This began the Romanov dynasty, which lasted for more than 300 years until the entire royal family was executed during the Bolshevik Revolution. However, between 1613 and 1917, other events took place that made it clear that Russia was, at heart, just like all of the other European countries. These events included a vicious revolt in 1670-1671 that the peasants, like all of Europe's peasants, were unable to sustain. Between 1689-1725, Peter I (the Great) ruled Russia. Peter was the first Russian ruler to travel abroad and was convinced that Russia needed to westernize to the greatest extent possible. Under Peter, Russia gave notice that it intended to become a dominant European power. Like the western leaders of his time, Peter consolidated his power by controlling the nobility and subordinating the church to the will of the state. Russia's other great ruler was Catharine II (the Great, 1762-1796). Catharine, a supposedly enlightened ruler, made concessions to the nobility and convoked a legislative commission that represented all classes except the serfs. In fact, serfdom reached its cruelest stage of development under Catharine's rule. Power to the elite and poverty to the masses is what enlightened Europeans, east and west, are all about.

Thus, as of circa 1800, even though it was the dominant power in Eastern Europe, Russia was a backward country when compared to most of the countries in western Europe. At what point then, did Russia become a world power? There is no evidence that anything of momentous proportions happened during the 1800s. In fact, Russia ended the 1800s by suffering a devastating military defeat at the hands of Japan, which could not be called a military power by any stretch of the imagination. Between 1900 and 1914, Russia was experiencing the internal turmoil that led to the Bolshevik Revolution. Certainly Russia could not have evolved into a world power during this period. And, as soon as the tzar was overthrown, the Russian revolution was mired in confusion and betrayed.

Then came Josef Stalin, who ignored external affairs and concentrated on eliminating his internal enemies. In the midst of all of this confusion and self-destruction, how Russia could have emerged from World War II as a world power is a mystery to me.

In fact, Russia never became a legitimate world power. However, it was recognized and treated as such because of several factors. These include:

(1) The Bolshevik Revolution. Western Europeans saw an economic ideology (state capitalism) emerge that could challenge their own. However, because the aims of the Bolshevik Revolution were so well promulgated as "communism," Russia effectively presented itself as a communist country. This gave Russia a degree of legitimacy among impoverished nations that had been abused and exploited by Western Europe. If impoverished nations and Russia were to form effective alliances, they would be able to dictate a new world economic and political order. Westerners had to placate Russia to keep this from happening.

(2) The German defeat in Russia. Russia used the same tactic against Germany that "defeated" Napoleon more than a hundred years earlier--- "avoid a major battle and wait until winter comes." Winter came, winter defeated the German army, the Russian army got the credit, and western Europeans were reminded of the difficulty of invading Russian territory.

(3) Russia's huge population and land mass. An elitist group that controlled that many people and such a huge expanse of land had to be accorded a degree of respect. Their potential could not be ignored.

(4) The possibility of a Russian-Chinese alliance. The west could not trust the likelihood that Russia and communist China would remain enemies. The key to keeping Russia and China apart was treating Russia as an equal.

(5) Russia's hot air. Russian elites knew how to talk a threatening game. They recognized their potential as an enemy of the west, and they played on that potential to the max. They issued hostile and threatening statements, even when they knew they were unable to back up what they said. As long as the west caved in to their demands, the Russians continued to talk the talk of a world power and be recognized as such.

(6) Russia's space program. Russia's emergence as the front-runner in space exploration was proof that they possessed the attributes that characterize a world power. The elites of the west projected the same attributes to all of Russia's institutions, including the military. The fact of the matter was quite different.

The tug of war between the east (symbolized by Russia) and the west (symbolized by the United States) does not present an option for oppressed people in the world. White power is the objective of both. People of color, particularly Black People, must recognize them for what they are: OUR ENEMIES.

"THE POPE" [The Papacy]

Where did "The Pope" come from, and what is the basis of "The Pope's" power? Why do so many people follow "The Pope" and adjust their lives in order to be in accordance with what "The Pope" decrees? What is this thing called "The Pope", how is it mixed in with the overall concepts of religion and white power and what does it mean to the quality of life of Black People throughout the world?

At the time of Jesus Christ, there was no such thing as "The Pope." Almost one thousand years later, there was still no such thing as "The Pope." Therefore, "The Pope" as people currently know it, is a relatively recent addition to history. As we move into the year 2000, "The Pope" has been around for only about 1000 years. Modern Christianity, on the other hand, has been around for 2000 years, Greek Orthodox Christianity has been around hundreds of years longer and African Christianity goes much farther back into antiquity. If "The Pope" is so essential to the religious well being of the world's people, why were people able to get along for so long without him? A study of "The Pope" provides Us with a model of how "elites" exploit the weaknesses and despair of human beings. The history of "The Pope" is tied into the development of Rome and the spread of the Roman Empire. Let's take a look at what happened.

The Romans were a fusion of people, mainly Etruscans, who settled around present day Italy at around 2000 BCE. They were very warlike and eventually gained control of Greek territories and formed the political structure called the empire. With the empire came the emperor, whose claim to legitimacy was partly linked to him being a descendant of God.

But then came the rise of European Christianity, which preached love for mankind and peace on earth. Christianity focused the attention of the masses on a God and taught the masses that God loved them in spite of their weaknesses, so the masses began to convert to Christianity in large numbers. This brought the Christian religion in direct conflict with the emperor and the might of the state. As a result, many of the early Christians were executed.

Still, many Roman citizens converted to Christianity. One of them, Paul, helped spread the religion. Under Paul's leadership, Christianity developed an organizational structure and, over time, established a monopoly in the printing industry.

The organizational structure consisted of independent churches, each governed by a clergy (board of elders) that got its "legitimacy" by falsely tracing itself to one of the original Apostles. One of the members of the board of elders frequently stood out and took the title of bishop. As religious rituals became more and more lavish, the lie that the 12 apostles were the first clergymen was fabricated in order to justify the development of a man-made priesthood. Bishops assumed leadership over the priesthood, and bishops in large cities took on more prestige than bishops in smaller cities. Not surprisingly, the bishop of Rome was the most visible bishop of all and became the most prestigious bishop of all.

Within two centuries, Christianity had become the official religion of the Roman Empire. All other religions were banned. Later, when the Roman Empire got weaker and was split into two divisions, Rome's emperors were unable to exert any authority over Rome's bishops, and the bishops began exercising many of the emperor's functions. With the passage of more time and further weakening of the empire, the church was left as the only institution of social control. The church, in many regards, became the government.

But just as importantly, the church was able to gain control of the very expensive printing industry. At that time, printing was so expensive that few could afford to have it done or open a printing business. Since the Church collected tithes/taxes and generated huge sums of income, it was able to assume control of the printing industry and establish a literary and artistic monopoly. From then on, the term "literature" was a code word for religious gospels and writings that supported the teachings of Christianity. For more than a thousand years, practically all of the writings that were made available to the public were produced by the church in the interest of the church. There was no freedom of expression; practically the only word the people read was the church's word.

As the years passed, it became clear that the churches controlled the people and the bishops controlled the churches, but the question was "Who should control the bishops?" The highest bishops in certain cities began to take on flattering titles, but the bishop of Rome took the blasphemous title of "papa" or "father," which was later modified into pope. The bishops at Rome and Constantinople, the second most important city, argued over which of them should be designated head of the church. The bishop of Rome won and in the 11th century the title of pope was reserved for the bishop of Rome.

Before proceeding, a few things need to be clarified. #1 Religion, white people's style, was controlled and administered by the emperor before there was any such thing as a priesthood and long before the office of "The Pope" was fabricated. Thus, organized religion was serving a political function, not a spiritual one. [In fact, organized religion and politics had the same game plan and the same objectives-- (a) both wanted to get undeserved money from the people (b) both wanted to control the people by keeping them passive and obedient (c) both realized the need to convince the people that they had the authority to get the people's money and keep the people passive and obedient and (d) both linked their legitimacy to a higher being]; #2 When the Roman empire began to deteriorate, the organized church assumed political functions that a truly religious body would not have assumed. As political power declined and church power ascended, each realized the key to its success. Politicians realized it was best for them to base their legitimacy on laws that are man-made, while leaders of organized religion realized that they could continue to base their legitimacy on laws they claim were declared by a higher being; #3 By the time the office of "The Pope" was fabricated, the organized church was more concerned about performing political functions than spiritual ones; and #4 The title of pope, meaning father or papa, is a blasphemous title because, according to Jesus Christ, only his Father is worthy of that name/title.

Based solely on what has been said up to this point, it is clear that not only is "The Pope" a religious fraud, the religion he purports to represent is fraudulent as well. First, the churches linked themselves to certain apostles in order to make the people more receptive to their claims of legitimacy. (The apostles themselves never claimed or gained any holy legitimacy.) Then, as the church became more organized, a church clergy developed. To legitimize this flim-flam clergy, it was claimed that the apostles were the original clergy and the church was only continuing that holy tradition.

When liars lie and when liars conspire, humanity is betrayed and people suffer haphazardly. When conspiring liars assume influence and power, social development is undermined and people suffer systematically. Such is part of the anatomy and function of both the state and church in the white world.

In the 11th century the title of Pope was reserved for the bishop of Rome. As the pope/papacy increasingly became a center of political power, its economic essence led to the inauguration of a tax system that was so intense the pope was accused of greed. Simultaneously, on other fronts, a papal mystique was being manufactured. For instance, "The Pope" became an intermediary between humans and God, "The Pope's" proclamations became divine, and rebelling against "The Pope" became the equivalent of rebelling against God. Later "The Pope" was declared beyond the judgment of anyone and began to take on dictatorial-like powers: only he could depose and restore bishops; only he could make new laws; only he could call general councils; only he could implement or revise religious law; only he could revise his own judgments; etc. Yes, "The Pope" became worthy of having his feet kissed, and people kissed them.

In a nutshell, that is the story of the development of "The Pope." 2000 years ago there was no such thing. 1000 years ago the title was minor but much discussed. But then, those who put their energy and money where their mouth was began to get their way, and "The Pope" began receiving recognition as God's intermediary on earth. It is incredible to think that intelligent humans beings could be duped into believing in such a sham, but the facts speak for themselves. What a blow to human advancement! What an epitaph for human intelligence!

I will not delve into the roles of "The Pope" or the church in the destruction of Black civilization, nor will I discuss how they are presently helping to transform Black People from a race of geniuses to a loose aggregation of inferiors. Let it suffice to say that "The Pope," like all the other bastions of white power that are discussed in this essay, prays for nothing but hard times when it comes to Black People. When Black individuals function intelligently, they not only let "The Pope" know that he can go to Hell, they do everything they can to send him there.

CONCLUSION

The purpose of this essay on "Europe" is to provide some basic information about white people. It is important to know your enemies, not simply in a vague, general manner, but in specific terms and within specific parameters. As Cheikh Anta Diop clearly demonstrated in THE CULTURAL UNITY OF BLACK AFRICA, there are qualities and quantities that are characteristic of white people wherever they may be. Wherever they may be found, they possess a generally consistent world-view and a generally consistent manner of functioning and relating to others. For Black People, the white world-view and the white manner of functioning and relating to others has translated into hundreds of millions of Black deaths and the trivialization of Black civilization. Unless We begin to effectively defend Ourselves against white power and white power advocates, the deaths and trivialization will continue to the point where Black People will be stripped of Our essence and drained of Our spirituality, Our Blackness.

PLAYING BLACK CHEAP

Do Black People really want to integrate with Europeans or their descendants? In case some Black individuals do, I will recap what has been stressed in this series.

The history of white people makes their priorities clear to any one who is not wearing blinders. When it comes to the privileges of the elite versus the rights of the common person, the privileges of the elites reign supreme. When it comes to the profits of status quo businesses versus the rights of the citizenry, the profits of status quo businesses get priority. Thus, the priorities of white people do not revolve around the well being of as many people as possible, as should be the case. In fact, among white people, the exact opposite is true. Establishing and maintaining the well being of as few individuals and businesses as possible is at the core of white culture, society and government. Black People need to be aware of that reality and opposed to it.

Among white people, JUSTICE is valued and much talked about, but unless one has money or "status," one cannot count on getting justice. LIBERTY is also valued and much talked about, but only those who march according to the status quo beat can hope to experience any degree of "liberty." And LIFE is valuable, as long as you belong to an elite group. Otherwise, life is cheap. For that reason, the law supports the members of the elites who abuse the common person, force the common person to work for pennies, overcharge the common person, drive the common person to the point of misery and desperation and force the common person into poverty, declining health and premature death. For that same reason, it is "against the law" for the common person to fight back in the most effective manner. The common person must fight back according to the laws that favor the elites; laws that are meant to protect the elite against the common person and maintain the elites' "right" to take advantage of the common person. The imbalance that this arrangement generates will forever resist the type of social equality Black People want to establish. Therefore, We should shun any system that supports that type of imbalance.

Black People should accept the fact that white people are not going to function in the interest of humanity as We perceive it. White people do not care about HUMANITY; at least, not in the same sense Black People do. For white people, humanity does not include all of the world's people. For white people, humanity does not include people of color. As a matter of fact, for white people humanity does not include most white individuals. Humanity, to white people, is composed of a small group of individuals who believe in elitist principles, acquire elitist status and insist on the right of the elites to continue abusing the masses and thriving at the expense of the masses. As long as that type of mindset rules, an inequality will exist that will keep the world in turmoil.

What do white people really care about? White people care about being in control and dictating all of the meaningful terms. That is a constant wherever white people are found. Whether or not they are worthy of being in control is of no consequence to them. To them, a system that is controlled by inept and maladjusted whites is better than one that is controlled by highly qualified non-whites. Why?

Because they know that a system will favor the abilities and inclinations of a specific group of people. They know that a system is not impartial and does not treat everybody equally. They know that a system is replete with biases that will promote the aspirations of people with certain types of tendencies and hinder the aspirations of equally capable people who possess different types of tendencies. They know that a system is both a tool and a weapon, and they want the system that governs them to be biased in their favor. At no time do they want to be governed by a system that favors the inclinations of a non-white group. That would make them a minority.

Minorities are doomed to fight uphill battles that they are unlikely to win. White people want to win!

As this essay has made clear, white people are always at odds with each other. The Romans were always at war with other Romans and whites outside of Rome. The Germans were always at odds with white Germans and white non-Germans. The same can be said of all of the others, like the Danes, French, English, Spanish, etc. But as much as they fuss and fight among and between themselves, they would rather see either of them in power than neither of them in power. That is because the differences that keep them at each other's throats are of a non-essential nature. They all function according to the same basic principles, and they all fit comfortably within the same basic system. Black People have to recognize that.

The white masses, the non-elites, have proven themselves incapable of effectively opposing their elites. Why? Because the individuals who make up the white masses are not fundamentally opposed to "the system," their problem is with their status (or lack thereof) within "the system." They believe in the white power system, and therefore do not want to change it appreciably. If a researcher begins with rebellions that took place from the early period of the Roman empire and continues through the modern era, s/he cannot find proof of substantial changes brought on by the activities of the white masses. Even the much heralded French and American revolutions failed to demonstrate the ability of the white masses to bring about worth-while changes. The only masses to benefit from the French Revolution were the slaves in San Domingo. The American Revolution, on the other hand, was not even a mass movement because it pitted white elites in England against white elites in the English colonies.

After all is said and done, the bottom line remains the same: white people are white people and white people, even the ones who call themselves liberals and socialists, are white power advocates. As humankind moves into the 21st century, white people and white governments have begun to realize that they cannot impose their system onto others as easily as they once could. As a result, they have shown a greater willingness to let non-whites acquire elite status within a white power system. They have realized that it is to their advantage to accept non-whites who they can trust and convert them into white power advocates. This allows white power to take on a more colorful image, a less racist image, but it does not change white power at all. Underneath the image, white power and white people are as white-centric as they were 2000 years ago.

Black People should not use the "new look" of white power as an excuse for allying with whites, trusting them or taking the "easy" way out. We should not reformat Our opinion of or response to white power or white people simply because they are willing to let some of Us join their "gang." White people have been the equivalent of a human curse for thousands of years, and will continue to be so. In order to ensure the well being of Black People, Black People must work to install an economic and political system that revolves around Black Power principles and values. We must install a system that favors Our abilities, inclinations and tendencies, a system that will be Our tool and Our weapon, a system that will intuitively represent the interests of Black People. Unequivocally, and without feeling the need to justify Our actions to others, We must be about the business of independence; of building a Black nation and establishing a Black government. If We do anything less than that, We will be playing Ourselves cheap, deceiving Ourselves and leaving Ourselves vulnerable to the whims of white people and white power.

The question has to be asked, over and over, "Are African-Americans taking too much for granted?" Are African-Americans making safe decisions, decisions that will be good for generations and generations of Black People? Are African-Americans recognizing that their only reliable source of salvation is internal and using that recognition to err on the side of caution?

To see this flag in color and order it go online to: http://asetbooks.com/Us/Mall/Blackidentityitems.html

IS INTEGRATING WITH WHITE PEOPLE A HEALTHY SOLUTION?

THE BLACK JEFFERSONIANS

Thomas Jefferson is one of the most popular persons in the historical annals of the United States of America. Mr. Jefferson was incredibly intelligent and augmented that intelligence with one of the best educations his time could offer. Mr. Jefferson is credited with being the author of the Declaration of Independence and a horde of other relatively progressive documents, and founder of the University of Virginia-- and he served two terms as the President of the United States. He was a gentleman in the true southern sense of the word, and epitomized everything that was desirable in a person with class. Jefferson's taste·was impeccable, his associates relatively reputable, his library impressive, his art collection enviable. He was not only sought after and esteemed by his contemporaneous peers, but has been revered through the ages as well. He was successful, he had status, he was famous and he excelled. He boldly faced life's challenges and often turned them to his advantage.

Thomas Jefferson might well have been the most hypocritical person to ever step foot in the state of Virginia. Mr. Jefferson was a sly, cunning and sinister racist, and he was able to camouflage his extreme racism so ingeniously that most persons were unable to detect his dire hatred of and spite toward people of color from Africa. But take note. The sister of Mr. Jefferson's wife was Black; she was also Mr. Jefferson's slave. The sister of Mr. Jefferson's wife was also Mr. Jefferson's concubine and the mother of several of Mr. Jefferson's children. Mr. Jefferson kept them all in slavery! Even as he lay dying, Mr. Jefferson refused to free his own flesh and blood!

Mr. Jefferson publicly expressed the opinion that he wanted the slaves to have all of the liberties and opportunities that other people had, but he was firmly against any effort to make liberty and equality a reality for Black People. In the face of overwhelming evidence to the contrary, Mr. Jefferson refused to recognize the fundamental humanity and intelligence of Black People. He privately urged those who sought his advice to hold their slaves in bondage and to control them forcefully. To Mr. Jefferson, the slaves were an indispensable source of labor; they were the key to maintaining the southern way of life and the key to his personal comfort. He would do all in his power, in his own underhanded and sinister way, to make sure that this peculiar institution, his peculiar institution, was not unduly tampered with. Even though slavery was an evil (which Jefferson publicly acknowledged), he privately made it clear that he was better off with it than without it.

Pyre!

Thomas Jefferson is disturbingly representative of an increasing number of Black persons. Such Black individuals, I will call them Black Jeffersonians for the sake of accuracy, are, like their role model, hypocritical, sinister, well-educated, reprehensible toward the mass of Black People and convinced that they have the right to make personal gains at the expense of less fortunate persons of color. They have a Jeffersonian approach to Black Nationalism, a Jeffersonian approach to everyday Black individuals, and a Jeffersonian approach to persons who legitimately try to represent the interests of Black People. The Black Jeffersonians not only think that they are superior to the Black crop, but distinct from it as well. In a manner of speaking, they are even more sinister than their unsuspecting mentor. After all, Black People could identify Mr. Jefferson as the enemy on sight, but the Black Jeffersonians look so much like other Black persons that they could pass for the real thing without being detected.

Nearly a century ago, W. E. B. DuBois had an image of Black individuals who would use their exceptional talents to help educate and lead Black People to equality and world respect. He referred to this group of exceptional individuals as the "talented tenth." The Black Jeffersonians have acquired the skills and knowledge needed to represent Black People in the manner Dr. DuBois had imagined, but they are not the least bit interested in doing so. Instead, they try to do such things as turn Black Studies into a purely academic "specialty" by eliminating its political relevance. They stress the intellectual nature of their work in order to side-step pressing political and social responsibilities. They profess their love for Malcolm X [because Malcolm X is dead!!]. But the most telling thing they do is say to themselves, "I cannot earn a lot of money or become famous if I represent the interests of Black People. Therefore I have to look for ways to de-emphasize and delegitimize the belief that I have a moral obligation to represent the interests of Black individuals who have been less fortunate than me."

So how do Black People recognize these Black Jeffersonians? Well, We can begin by looking at the faculty lists of America's most respected colleges and universities, all of which are white. If there is a name on those lists that represents a Black person, that person is quite probably a Black Jeffersonian. Then We can look at the enrollment lists of America's most respected colleges and universities. If there is a name on those lists that represents a person of color, that person is quite probably learning to be a Black Jeffersonian. We can also look at the alumni lists of America's most respected colleges and universities. If there is a name on those lists that represents a Black person, that person is quite probably a Black Jeffersonian. We can look at the wannabes on Black campuses and in status quo type institutions, because they have bought into a distorted reality of Black worth. We can also look at corporate America and check out the Black individuals who are being allowed to profit from the corporate game. We can peruse the status quo political scene and observe the Black individuals who play that game; they think they have established a place for themselves in America's power house. We can check out Black individuals who consider themselves highly educated, highly motivated and highly successful, because these are the persons who are most likely to adopt a philosophy of elitism and succumb to the power of self-interest. And, We can look at Black individuals who have crossed over to the white world in some regard; through marriage, entertainment success, athletic excellence, etc. They are often unable to distinguish between their myth and their reality or white people's myths and white people's reality.

John C. Calhoun, a staunch Jeffersonian and paragon of excellence and success, expressed the Jeffersonian concept quite precisely. Being a non-apologetic Jeffersonian, and therefore not an ideal role model for his chameleonic Black progeny, Calhoun made it clear that it is an inevitable law of society that one portion of the community must depend upon the labor (blood, sweat and tears) of another portion for its standard of living. Black Jeffersonians might use this logic to support their belief that they have a right to live comfortably at the expense of Black labor, Black integrity and Black tears. Daniel Webster, their southern and liberal crony from the north, certainly felt it to be appropriate. That's why he would stand in the rain and make a liberal speech while a Black person held an umbrella over his head. Black Jeffersonians must feel that they deserve to be accorded as much deference as Mr. Webster was accorded.

Pyre!

The talented tenth in the Black community is not the group of people Dr. DuBois had envisioned. The present group of talented persons would be more properly called the treacherous tenth, because their objective is not to help the mass of Black People but to take advantage of them. These persons prostitute themselves in order to get some white money and white recognition, but genuinely talented persons are unwilling to demean themselves simply for the sake of profit or fame. Nor are genuinely talented persons willing to demean others simply for the sake of profit or fame. Therefore, the real talented tenth in the Black community is made up of those who are in the ghettoes and Black neighborhoods working to help Us progress as a race of People. They are persons who have refused to sell out to white power and, as a result, are experiencing greater personal and financial hardships than they would otherwise be experiencing. They are not the success stories that America likes to parade before Us, but they are the persons who Black People will celebrate once We reacquire the respect of the world. To hell with those like-white successful Blacks who aspire to white standards. We, the masses of Black People, are better off without them. We are better off without them and their sang-froid quest for a life of luxury.

Luxury. The extreme accumulation of wealth. The vicious hoarding of goods and services that less fortunate individuals need in order to survive and live decently. Don't talk to me about the horrors of war and racial confrontation, talk to me about the horrors of luxury, its violent nature, its inhumane consequences. Talk to me about the more than 35,000 children who needlessly suffer and die every day because legal thieves are hoarding goods and services. Talk to me about the hundreds of millions of persons who suffer excruciating physical pain, mental distress and spiritual malaise because luxury has put a dollar and cents price tag on medical attention and "the pursuit of happiness." Rich people "live the life" and are the source of wonderful images, but the damage they generate is so efficient, so immense, so viciously destructive. Humankind would be much better off without them.

Each and every Black individual has a choice to make. Each of Us can either serve a Black master or serve a white master. If We serve a Black master, then We commit Ourselves to the uplift and betterment of the mass of Black People. If We serve a white master, then We do anything but commit Ourselves to the betterment and uplift of the Black masses. Black intellectuals are trying to trick Black People; they serve the white world but give lip service to Black Power. Their feather heavy sentiments ache for Black People, their public posturing makes that perfectly clear; but they are better rewarded by white power's resources and money. So, merrily they go in support of the white power structure.

Black People should not waste time trying to reform persons like the Black Jeffersonians. John Hammonds, the esteemed South Carolina congressman from Massachusetts, articulated the Jeffersonian will to persevere more than 150 years ago. He made it more than clear that slavery was not going to be abolished by appeals to the slaveholders; not to their consciences, not to their hopes, not to their fears nor to their interests. White people's status, he continued, their honor, their legitimacy and their right to exploit Black People were approved by nature and God, and nothing could change that. The Black Jeffersonians would insist on their "rights" just as forcefully, but in a deceitful, off-handed way.

The Black Jeffersonians are not motivated to contribute to the well-being of the Black masses. That is understandable because they are weak links in an otherwise strong Black chain. The Black Jeffersonians have placed all of their energy into promoting and defending the white power structure. That, again, is understandable because they are too weak to imagine themselves building anything of value. Fortunately, the fact that they are weak does not mean that Black People are handcuffed by their shortcomings. We can do better without them than with them.

PLAYING BLACK CHEAP

Can These Colors Merge:
Where Did The Idea Of Integration In America Come From?

Where did the idea of integration in the United States come from? When Black People were on the African continent, they were not thinking about integrating with white people. When Black People were attacked by slave traders and slave hunters, they were not thinking about integrating with white people. When Black People were packed like sardines in those ships sailing across the Atlantic Ocean, they were not thinking about integrating with white people. When Black People were being fondled and inspected in those slave houses, they were not thinking about integrating with white people. When Black People were standing on that auction block and listening to white people bid for them, they were not thinking about integrating with white people. When Black People were taken to white people's plantations and forced to work for free, they were not thinking about integrating with white people. When Black People watched other Black men and women being whipped and lynched for rebelling against their enslavers, they were not thinking about integrating with white people. When Black People watched their families being separated at the whim of white "masters," they were not thinking about integrating with white people. When Black People broke hoes and spit in white people's food, they were not thinking about integrating with white people. When Black People ran off to the swamps and became maroons, they were not thinking about integrating with white people. When Black People rebelled against the slave condition, they were not thinking about integrating with white people. When Black People like Gabriel Prosser, Denmark Vezey and Nat Turner planned to take over white states, they were not thinking about integrating with white people. When Black People heard about the Dred Scott decision, they were not thinking about integrating with white people. When Black People realized that a war between the states was about to begin, they were not thinking about integrating with white people. And, when Black People walked off the plantations and freed themselves during the War Between the States, they were not thinking about integrating with white people. Where, then, did this idea of integration in the United States come from?

Was integration a Black idea? If it was, then when was it born? and why didn't We think about it when We were the only ones concerned about Our plight? If integration was a Black idea, why wasn't it a cornerstone of the Black Abolitionist Movement, and why wasn't it discussed by the Brothers and Sisters who were plotting to overthrow the slave system?

Did white people in America come up with the idea of integration? Is that why they went to Africa looking for slaves; because they knew they would want some former slaves to integrate with a few hundred years down the road? Is that why white people are so much against what they call "miscegenation;" because they want each member of the "integrated society" to be clearly white or clearly Black? Is that why white people wrote the slave codes; so that Black People would be well aware of all of Our rights as an equal member of society? I don't think so.

So where did this idea of integration come from? Please, don't mention the Constitution, the Bill of Rights, the Declaration of Independence or any other such European document. There is no mention of integration in any of those documents. Nothing is in any of them that even suggests that Black People and white people should live together as equals in this country.

Integration is, pure and simple, one of Nature's options. Any time members of different races or entities meet or come together, regardless of the circumstances, Nature factors in integration as one of a myriad of possibilities. In this particular case, the case of Blacks and whites in the United States of America, Nature factored in the possibility of integration. But in the world of human politics, natural possibilities carry less weight than a feather. None of the humans involved seriously thought about integration as a solution to the problem of white/Black relations in the United States because it was an impossible solution.

And then came the white abolitionist movement. Were white abolitionists thinking about integrating with Black People? Not at all. But something was wrong! The Black Abolitionist Movement was exposing the lack of conviction of white abolitionists; it had to be undermined. The solution was to get Black individuals to present their cause under the sponsorship of white abolitionists. All of a sudden, certain Blacks and certain whites were working together and getting to know each other better (on white terms). The whites remained staunch in their opposition to integration, but some Blacks were beginning to spend more time looking at the possibility of Nature's impossible solution.

And then came the Civil War. At its end, two indisputable realities loomed large. Number one, Black People had freed themselves. Number two, white northerners were afraid to trust white southerners with power. As a result, whites made Black People citizens of the United States, gave Black People the right to vote and created a virtual political reality, an artificially integrated political and social environment called Reconstruction. The whites remained staunch in their opposition to integration, but certain Black persons became convinced that integration was not an impossible solution after all.

But certain Black persons were wrong. They and some reactionary whites began trying to sell the idea of integration to the Black masses, but that idea was and still is wrong. Integration is not the solution to race relations in the United States. We must understand that integration was a remote blip on the screen of the white abolitionist movement. White abolitionists never dreamed of actually integrating with Black People. Integration, within the Black community, was an eccentric afterthought of a small number of Blacks who did not recognize that white abolitionists were using them to achieve goals that were of benefit to white people, not Black People. Blacks and whites working together was a means that made it easy for whites to reach their goal, nothing more. For white northerners, integration was a political weapon used to control white southerners immediately after the Civil War. Integration was never viewed as a viable solution to the resolution of the race issue. Thus, integration was an idea that was hardly imagined, a fetus that was never conceived, and the basis of a virtual political reality called Reconstruction. Reconstruction was not a real political reality, it was a virtual political reality. Reconstruction went up in smoke in 1877, as it was supposed to do, and integration went up in smoke along with it. But exasperated Black individuals who felt they had nowhere else to call home and nothing else to hold on to, grabbed a handful of that smoke and refused to let it go.

For the nearly 150 years since then, certain Black persons have been holding on to that hand full of nothing gone up in smoke. As soon as Black People garner the strength to open their hands and see that there is nothing there, Black People can begin struggling within a different context. We made a mistake when We jumped on the integration bandwagon. We have contributed a lot of blood, lives, sweat, tears, energy, money and belief in this idea, but it is time to reassess the situation and admit that We made a mistake! We need to change the context within which We are struggling; to forget about integration and civil rights and focus Our attention on Black Nationalism. Within that context We can successfully reach the goal that is at the heart of Our struggle-- EQUALITY.

It was clear that, over time, Black People and white people had become different sides of the same coin, a very unlikely coin. In that regard, the two are bound together somewhat forever. But that does not require that the two sides lose their separate identities or merge into a singularity. We are not like Siamese twins. Each side can safely and securely go its own way. The only attribute the two side must have is equal value. Equality for Black People and white people equates to political independence for each.

We made a mistake, a 150 year-long mistake; but you don't stay in a mess simply because you have invested a lot of time and energy in it. Once you realize the mistake will continue to harm you, you pull yourself together, figuratively go back to where you were before you made the mistake, and take the road that you should have taken all along.

There are a lot of Black individuals who are trying to save themselves by continuing to sell the myth of integration to succeeding generations of Black youth. But under circumstances where progress for one group always equates to problems for the other group, integration is practically impossible. Within Nature's scheme of things, a merger of these two "colors" might be possible. Unfortunately, it is a human scheme of things that We are dealing with. We need to deal intelligently.

Integration: A Huge Mountain to Climb

Integration is not primarily a matter of physics, integration is primarily a matter of chemistry. At one extreme, all Black persons could live in one part of the country while all white persons live in the other part of the country, and almost complete integration could be realized; whereas at the other extreme a consistent pattern of "salt and pepper" residential areas and business offices could be part and parcel of an almost totally segregated society. Integration is not primarily a matter of physics, integration is primarily a matter of chemistry.

At no time in history has a white population integrated with another population of people.

All humans are self-absorbed... to a degree. Human beings are primarily concerned about themselves, first as individuals and secondly in terms of the extent to which individuals assign value to other individuals. In fact, if there are four laws of human nature that drive individuals, they would likely be:

(1) self survival or self preservation; (2) self enjoyment; (3) be your brother's keeper, but at a distance; and (4) ignore law #3 whenever your conscience or some other plausible consideration will allow it. Each individual is almost mandated by Nature to pursue the first two laws, at least to the extent that survival and pleasure are immediate objectives that call for immediate resolution. The third law speaks to that something about humankind that makes us capable of moral behavior, and the fourth law speaks to that something about humankind that militates against the intrusion of moral responsibility. The fourth law represents the power of that basic human instinct that goes against being obligated; obligated to help others, obligated to

care about others, obligated to spend time doing one thing when doing something else is more to one's liking, etc. Being self-absorbed is simply not compatible with being obligated in regard to someone else.

Human nature is not in sync with the intrusion of ideological entities such as morality. Therefore, humans are incapable of moderating their basic instincts unless they have been subjected to thousands of years of civilization. White people have not realized that civilization advantage yet.

Civilization is not innate to humans. Human beings do not have a "do the right thing" gene. It has not been established that human beings will tend to act in a socially responsible manner when given the opportunity to do so. Quite to the contrary, what has been determined is that human beings, when confronted with the threat of penalty, will act in an irresponsible manner less frequently. However, their default manner of behavior continues to be governed by the four human laws that were stated earlier. Those laws resist socially progressive efforts among persons/groups who view themselves as equals. Certainly, those laws are a greater obstruction to socially progressive efforts among persons/groups who consider themselves "different" in one way or another.

Humans are incapable of moderating their basic instincts unless they have been subjected to thousands of years of civilization. White people have not realized that civilization advantage yet. In addition, white people perceive that there is at least one basic difference between them and Black People. White people believe that they are better than Black People; that because of the difference(s), Black People are not the "equal" of white people. The third law, "be your brother's keeper, but at a distance," cannot apply to "black-white relations" because white people do not view Black People as their brothers. This manner of feeling generates a chemical drift that favors incompatibility over compatibility. In other words, if white people and Black People are "mixed," the mixture is more likely to be explosive than affirmative; more likely to be hostile than affectionate.

It has been stated that human nature is a deterrent to integration. It has also been stated that lack of civilization is a deterrent to integration. And, it has been stated that perceived differences are a deterrent to integration. Such deterrents are oh so potent, oh so influential.

The Human Reality

The conclusion white people reached about integration is correct, you know. It is what led them to their conclusion that is wrong. The concept of integration runs much deeper than We have imagined, because equals neither seek nor need to integrate. When equals contact each other, they either blend as a matter of course, interrelate as a matter of course, or carry out their separate functions as a matter of course. They are able to proceed "as a matter of course" because neither party doubts its own nor the other party's equality. Integration, therefore, manifests itself as a matter of course; its occurrence does not require notation. If "integration" becomes an issue, particularly within conflictive parameters, the fundamental question is not integration at all, but perceived differences that are beyond the norm. These type differences are what Blacks and whites in the United States cannot come to grips with.

In order for Black People and white people to integrate, they must first perceive each other as equals.

Black People and white people belong to the same natural species. In that regard the two are equal. Only the first law should serve as a major barrier to a blending of the two. However, the human perspective is not as mature or sensitive as that of Mother Nature, but it is the human perspective that determines conscious human responses. From the human perspective, Blacks and whites differ fundamentally in color, culture and cosmogeny. Their views of the world and of each other are fundamentally discordant. Their institutions are buttressed by contrary pillars, particularly the intangible ones (the most important ones). In the absence of a long standing civilizing agent, at least one of the two groups will remain incapable of making the adjustments that must precede integration.

Within a progressive social order, the civilizing process would be one of the concerns of the government. In the United States, government is often mentioned, but there is no concrete evidence of its existence. What rules is the political system. Neither government nor politics is a pursuit human beings have a natural inclination for; remember, humans are self absorbed--- they are inside of themselves. Politics and government require that the individual emerge from within himself and partially submerge himself into abstract ideologies and other individuals. Self-survival? Sure, but in a much too distant context for most individuals. Self-enjoyment? I think not.

The rub is that politics and government are key elements if Black and white people in the United States have any hope of integrating. Politics is important because politics governs white life, and white life is the dominant force in the world today. In order to neutralize white domination, a counter-political force has to be created that can frustrate the political status quo. After the political status quo has been frustrated, a new governmental entity has to be installed and made dominant. Government, because it seeks harmony among its constituents, allows for the possibility of integration. But to expect government to actually produce an integrated social order is to rely on a long shot, to say the least; even under almost ideal conditions. Under present conditions, to expect an integrated social order to evolve is simply ludicrous.

It is ironic but understandable that Black People in the United States, not white people, seek integration. It is ironic because white people have more to gain from integration than Black People. For starters, white people simply cannot dominate Black People for long; the artificial barriers they use to cripple Black People always prove incapable of sustaining themselves. Plus, white people do not have what it takes to successfully compete with Black People over an extended period of time; whites cannot access the advantages of civilization that are available to Black People. And, whites are so full of themselves that they do not realize that the rest of the world is not at their arbitrary disposal and not seeking their approval. Whites have incredibly warped perceptions of human reality and non-white energy, and those warped perceptions will cost whites dearly in the long run.

Integration is a mountain that is too huge for white people to climb. In the process of spending so much time and energy trying to force whites to climb that mountain, Black People have frowned upon a noble path, that of separation. In the process of separating from white people, We can begin to integrate with the quietly emerging new world racial order that is already imposing itself on the United States and other bastions of white power. That is the kind of mix that would be good for Black People and the rest of the world.

On the Way to the Nuthouse

Final Words

PLAYING BLACK CHEAP

Introduction

Psychologically speaking, it is normal for a person to be somewhat abnormal because the other extreme of "normal" is "perfect", and none of us is perfect. As a matter of fact, we are all closer to being "deranged" than perfect. In the case of Black People, the quality of being abnormal is present, but not just for the usual reasons. Thus, Black Psychology is the study of the unusual factors that enhance, augment and make unique the abnormality of Black individuals.

To deal adequately with this subject We must understand (1) the subconscious and (2) the conscious. In the process of acquiring this understanding, We will realize that Black individuals are trying to move in opposite directions at the same time, and are seeking goals that are mutually exclusive. Frantz Fanon, through his masterful writing entitled Black Skin White Masks, will help Us get to the root of this internal tug of war.

Let's begin, however, by getting some working definitions of the entities "the subconscious" and "the conscious."

What Is Inside of Us Surrounds Us

When we speak of what is inside of Black individuals, we are speaking the language of psychology, and we are restricting the contents to what is relevant to an introductory essay such as this. As such, we are prepared to recognize three entities; the subconscious, the conscious and the super-conscious. Of these three, we will address primarily the first two.

The subconscious is that portion of Our being that precedes personal awareness. The subconscious triggers unsolicited responses to what We contemplate and to what affects Us deeply by generating feelings and sensations. The subconscious is similar to a primeval operating system that is full of data accumulated over the ages, and contains basic instructions that suggest what Our response to certain stimuli should be. The subconscious nurtures and protects Our concept of self, reaffirms the validity of Our customs, monitors Our drives for love, companionship and recognition, and protects a society's "collective ego." The subconscious makes an impression on the individual but it does not frantically plead its case. Because it fails to frantically plead its case, the subconscious can be rather easy to ignore at decision-making time, and it often is. As We shall learn, to ignore the subconscious is a harmful activity.

The subconscious of African-Americans, for the most part, is normal. Even though Black People have been disrupted, hunted, enslaved, colonized and despised for centuries, this steady onslaught of negative signals has not been able to seriously disorient Our primeval operating system. Needless to say, the Black subconscious is very well protected; it has to be because it houses the best of what We have left of Ourselves.

The conscious part of Our being is also an operating system filled with data, but it is relatively recent data. The data that occupies the conscious is not time tested, it is random, and, most importantly, it is not necessarily fundamental. The conscious part of an individual's being is better known to that individual than the subconscious part. As a matter of fact, the individual is able to manipulate the conscious to the extent that he or she is aware of what is there (its contents) and how it got there (its genesis). Unfortunately, the conscious takes in so much data (everything that a person sees, hears, smells, touches, tastes) that an individual is aware of only a small portion of its contents (2 to 5 per cent) and practically none of the genesis of these contents. [This huge collection of unknown data in the conscious part of our being must not be confused with the data that precedes conscious awareness and occupies the subconscious part of Our being.]

The super-conscious is the deliberate projection of an ideal. The super-conscious is not an operating system at all, but an objective. The super-conscious of most Black individuals lacks real substance. It is vague and too unexplored to cross the bridge that separates the ideal from the physical. The Black super-conscious, for the most part, will not be addressed in this essay.

Individuals deliberately search the conscious part of their being for data that they can use to help them make choices and decisions. As they search, they are able to compare what they think they should do with what they want to do (if a conflict exists), and sensibly assess various alternatives. But there are serious limitations to be found here. As was just stated, most of the data in the conscious cannot be accessed because the individual is not aware of its existence. Additionally, there is an excess of unpleasant data in the Black conscious that is either "hidden," "forgotten" or "unacknowledged," and a host of other data that challenges the very foundation of the Black subconscious. For these reasons, we can state that the conscious portion of Black People's being is not only uniquely abnormal, but especially abnormal.

What is at the core of this unique abnormality? We can start by mentioning an inferiority complex that is not properly understood and therefore not properly addressed. We can follow that by exposing the roots of Black individual's fear of white people. And, We can add to those the churning conviction that We are failing to accomplish what We try so hard to accomplish. Let's cover these one at a time.

Black People have an inferiority complex. For the most part, Black individuals do not acknowledge this complex, and they are apt to attack anyone who suggests that it exists; but it exists and is alive and kicking. The mere fact that We try to "prove" so much to white people is proof not only that the inferiority complex exists, but that it dominates the conscious element of Our being. Yet, one thing needs to be made perfectly clear. As strange as it might sound, Black People do not believe that white people are "better" than We are. A large percentage of Black individuals honestly believe that Black People are just as smart as, if not smarter than, white individuals. A large percentage of Black individuals honestly believe that Black individuals are more attractive than white individuals. A large percentage of Black individuals honestly believe that, on an even field, Black individuals will outdo white individuals more often than not. A large percentage of Black individuals honestly believe that, in almost any comparison, a Black person's performance will either equal or exceed that of a white person. Yet, Black People bleach their skin, trim their lips and nose, treat their hair, desert their schools, forsake their own heritage, destroy their own institutions and seek the lightest mate available in order to imitate whites as much as possible. Given the opportunity, millions of Black individuals would imitate white people to no end! Why? Because Our inferiority complex, though real, is deceiving because it does not revolve around the expected genetic, biological or theoretical bases. The basis of Our inferiority complex is the undeniable fact that white people have dominated Us for as long as anyone can remember. We cannot escape that reality, and it keeps Us unsettled. Our conscious is not comfortable with that reality. However, Our conscious is not convinced enough of the gravity of that reality to deal with it, but Our subconscious is quite convinced. Our subconscious, therefore, keeps sending out messages to the effect that that inferiority complex must be invalidated.

But Black People's inferiority complex is based on a domination complex; therefore, what must be invalidated are not genetic, biological or theoretical claims but white people's domination of Black People. What a problem that poses because Black People do not want to take on a task such as that. How then is this domination complex to be invalidated? Sadly, Black individuals are trying to invalidate the complex without dealing with it as it should be dealt with. We invest Our time and energy in futile exercises. We continue to drown Ourselves in activities that disprove genetic, biological and theoretical claims of white superiority, force open white school doors, white bathrooms, and white whatevers, and dialogue about causes and effects of discrimination, etc. But they fail to eliminate that sense of inferiority because deep down inside, We know that We can only invalidate the white claim of superiority by challenging them in ways that raise the stakes and change the rules of the game. How to accomplish that goal without addressing it, that is the conundrum; and the source of Our inertia. We are reluctant to do what We know has to be done, but it has to be done nonetheless. Why? Because, in the final analysis, it is not whites that We have to convince of Our worth. Sooner or later We will have to convince Ourselves, and there is only one way We can do that.

Let's put what has just been said in a nutshell:

(1) Black People have an inferiority complex. (2) The Black subconscious insists that the inferiority com-

plex be invalidated. (3) The steps Black People are taking to invalidate the inferiority complex are not getting the job done because a domination complex is at its base. (4) In order to invalidate that domination complex, Black People have to challenge the power relationship between white people and Black People in a way that results in fundamental changes in the "rules of the game" that govern race relations. (5) Black People want the rules of the game changed but Black People don't want to take on the responsibility of changing them. The conundrum becomes, "How do We invalidate Our sense of inferiority while simultaneously failing to do what a deserving group of reasonable people would do?" (6) Blacks continue to shun their responsibility, whites continue to dominate Blacks, and the sense of inferiority remains (with its troublesome energy).

There We have it. Everyday Black individuals who want to take what they perceive as the "safe and easy" way out are unwittingly trying to manipulate their essential being. They are running into two problems: (1) they can only access a limited portion of their conscious being and (2) they cannot access their subconscious being at all. The result is that Black individuals are following a course of action that the conscious is not fully in accord with and the subconscious is completely opposed to, resulting in an individual who is at all times at odds with himself/herself, and individuals who are at all times engaging in activities that they know will not adequately address a critical need. The result: Black People's unusual state of psychological unhealthiness.

Our subconscious realizes that an inferiority complex challenges its very foundation. An inferiority complex challenges the very essence of Black People, and any such challenge must be eradicated. Additionally, the conscious portion of a normal human being cannot accept a challenge to the foundation of its very being. No normal human being can tolerate such an affront, and no human being who does can remain normal for long.

Let us move on.

As was stated earlier, the inferiority complex is only one entity that needs to be considered. There are other internal contradictions that are just as critical and disturbing. One involves an analysis of what is at the core of Black individuals' "fear" of white people. We don't want to admit that We are afraid of white people, but We need to (it could serve as a source of relief, psychologically speaking). The irony, though, is that We are not afraid of white people because We think they can outdo Us in a physical confrontation. Nor are We afraid of white people because of their military might. No, neither of those--- nor anything of the sort! In fact, if the truth be told, white people are Our scapegoats when the issue of "fear" is addressed. It is easy for Black People to point to white people's power as a deterrent to Black activism, much easier than admitting that what We are actually afraid of are Our own suspected shortcomings. What a burden it is to try to keep the world from discovering the "family secret;" the fact that, at this late date, Black individuals are still afraid to trust men and women who look just like Black individuals look. Frequently, We talk "trash" to each other about Our shortcomings, about how a "nigger" can't be trusted and about this negative and that negative, but We make such statements without really taking them to heart. We need to begin taking them to heart, because if they are true, We need to deal with them at the real level in order to iron them out, get them out of Our system and get them out of Our way.

But let's stay closer to the subject at hand. The essence of this "fear" element, that is what We need to explore. How can We genuinely value Ourselves if We doubt each other so profoundly? And it's not just that We doubt each other, but that We doubt each other's very qualities, each other's basic building blocks. To profess "X", believe the opposite of "X" and keep that contradiction buried deeply inside in such a race conscious environment has to produce a mental wound that consistently drips blood onto Our psyche. These drip-drops of blood, traits like doubt, depression, reluctance, indifference and a host of other negatives, manage to become dominant, and via such drops We are led right back to "individuals who are at odds with themselves." We are led to uncomplimentary conclusions about Ourselves, and are forced to entertain impressions that question Our "equality." We can't help but admit that it's not white people who are keeping Us "down," but Our own selves. We can't help but ask the question, "How can a people who are 'equal' continue to be burdened by the same old shortcomings over and over again, shortcomings that are not burdening Our competitors?" We are forever ill at ease inside, and Our subconscious will keep us ill at ease until acceptable resolutions are sought.

Frantz Fanon (p. 84, BLACK SKIN, WHITE MASKS) speaks of "the impossibility of explaining man outside the limits of his capacity for accepting or denying a given situation." The ability to accept and deny coupled with the inability to accept and deny define limits that are impossible to get "over, under, around or through." To accept, as a psychological reality, the domination of white people is totally unacceptable to Black People because it supports white people's insane claims of superiority, but to deny their dominance is just as unacceptable because their dominance is beyond doubt. And to deny that whites dominate Us because We allow them to is even more unacceptable because it ridicules Our intelligence. We are stuck, then, inside limits defined by uncomfortable parameters, limits that are unacceptable because they enslave Our spirit, keep Us from experiencing internal freedom, keep Us at odds with Ourselves as individuals and keep Us at odds with Ourselves as a People.

Again We see people who, individually and collectively, are at odds with themselves. We see people who, individually and collectively, are engaging in activities that they know will not adequately address critical needs. We see people, Black People, who are experiencing an abnormal state of psychological imbalance.

Finally, we will address the issue of failing to accomplish what We try so diligently to accomplish. We will label this "the frustration syndrome." This reality has definite psychological ramifications, but it is not a psychological issue per se. On close examination it becomes obvious that this is merely an issue of failing to struggle intelligently.

One thing should be made clear before moving on. We are not talking about individual failures in this section, even though many Blacks fail in business and social affairs because they are forced to endure circumstances and conditions that whites are not forced to endure. What we are talking about here are group failures; the failure to acquire genuine political power, the failure to get white people to recognize Us according to Our due, the failure to acquire equal access to goods and services, the failure to have adequate say-so in what the government does with Our money, the failure to expel blatant prejudices from the minds, hearts and laws of white America, the failure to gain equal access to employment opportunities, health care and housing facilities, the failure to make the progress We want so dearly to make, etc., etc., etc. No matter how hard Black People struggle to remove these products of a racist myth, they remain before Us, as strong an impediment as ever. And, worse still, no other group of people is willing to help Us get Our point across or give Us words of genuine encouragement. It is no wonder, then, that many of Us end up throwing Our hands in the air and asking, "Is it worthwhile to continue this fight against injustice?"

The fight against injustice is a worthwhile fight, even if We have to wage it alone. However, it is imperative that We wage that fight intelligently. Let's continue.

On page 140, Fanon mentions that Black People are "toys...in the white man's hands." Black People respond "to the world's anticipation." Trivial impressions have been implanted inside Us that give rise to behavior that defies logical analysis. A normal person in Our condition would not attempt to be objective, but We insist on being so. Instead of doing what We should do, We concentrate on trying to do what the world considers appropriate. Instead of doing what We should do, We fail to struggle intelligently. Why? Because (1) What the "world" thinks of Us is more important to Us than what We think of Ourselves, and (2) Doing what the "world" thinks should be done seems less dangerous. Let's address reason #1 first.

One can never feel secure when he or she has to guess what someone else's expectations are and act in accordance with those expectations. One is therefore filled with doubt! Black People are filled with doubt. We are like the third grade pupil who is trying to guess what the teacher wants him or her to say. We are not confident that We can guess correctly, and We are not sure if what We choose to say or do will be proper or "adequate". Our preference is to defer, to let someone "more capable" have a hand in the process, to "arrive" (Fanon) just as the world expects Us to "arrive." We don't have the confidence to do it alone, so We wait; for the courts, the President, any white person, the federal government or something of that ilk. We have a tendency to think that "something of that ilk" knows better than We do what is "right," and what the world expects of Black People.

However, the "world" does not have to suffer the consequences of Our failure to do what needs to be done. Black People alone suffer those consequences! Our frustration continues to increase, generating more pressure inside an already overloaded psyche, pressure that is impossible to contain. We relieve it, small portions at a time, by abusing each other. But We don't relieve it nearly as quickly as it accumulates, so it continues to do Us harm.

Reason #2 revolves around the safety argument. We do what the "world" thinks should be done because We think it is less dangerous. We think We will not incur the "world's" wrath (that is, the white world's wrath) if We try to make the world (white people) abide by the rules "the world" has laid out. Such rules are found in documents like the Bill of Rights and the Constitution. The fact of the matter is that Black People experience more harm playing according to white rules over an extended period of time than by bringing the issue to a head once and for all. The suffering caused by a bitter war over a short period causes less harm and damage than the suffering caused by luxury and oppression over a similar period of time. We have to think well enough to understand the validity of this concept, and act accordingly.

But We don't. Instead, We are like that hamster on the treadmill. We keep using all of that energy but, unlike the hamster, We know that We are going to achieve absolutely nothing? Why do We do it, over and over again!! That is the question that is driving Us to the nuthouse.

Allegorically speaking, Black People in the United States are in the midst of a group psychological breakdown. In the process of trying to accommodate white people, We have almost driven Ourselves crazy. If "every citizen of a nation is responsible for the actions committed in the name of that nation" (Fanon p. 91), then every so-called African American feels responsible for Our grand failure and carries the psychological weight of that failure. If there were an actual nuthouse for groups of people, We would need to admit Ourselves and go through an extensive period of rehabilitation.

Animals are imitators by nature. To imitate is the natural thing to do. Imitation over a period of time becomes habit. Habit over a period of time becomes custom, and customs are the building blocks of a social structure, a metaphysical reality. Unfortunately, that metaphysical reality for Black People has become characterized by deferring, defaulting, doubting, a reluctance to assert Ourselves, depression, and wanting to be recognized within the white context. Black, you understand, but within the white context.

Impossible, to be sure. But real!! Another anomaly (irregularity)! Black People's psyche seems to be wrapped in anomaly.

The key to eliminating the anomaly is to struggle within a context that can produce the result We so dearly want. (We do want what We say We want. Else, not having it wouldn't leave Us as sick as We are.) However, Black People's inferiority complex "is particularly intensified among the most educated" (Fanon (p. 25), those who would normally be expected to lead, recognize the need for a change and organize the people around a new course of action. So a different source of leadership must be sought. The solution lies with the Black person who has been least imposed on by the white world's standards. The solution lies with me and you, those persons whose "education" has not made them strangers unto themselves.

Conclusion

The subconscious and the conscious involve much more than the mind, which is exactly why the term "psychology" is appropriate. The spirit; therein We find the essence of psychology. Therein lies the complex maze of simple impulses that create the "balances" that are characteristic of a "normal" person and the excessive imbalances that are characteristic of an "abnormal" person. While the subconscious and the conscious are not always on the same page (working together in harmony), it is not normal for the two to be constantly at odds. The usual course of action is that the one responds and the other tries to either act in accordance or negotiate an acceptable compromise. It is at this point that the response of Black individuals is abnormal. Instead of trying to either act in accordance or negotiate an acceptable compromise with the Black subconscious, the Black individual (super-conscious) attempts to manipulate the Black conscious into delegitimizing the Black subconscious, to strip it of its worth, to declare it a bastard and render it null and void. At best, that can result in an increasingly unhealthy psyche. At worst, it can result in psychological and spiritual genocide.

Since neither of those is desirable, Black People must impose a healthy solution. As has been suggested all along, that solution begins with a basic change in the context within which We struggle.

The assertion that Black People can gain equality and respect through civil rightist and integrationist type activities is replete with fallacy. The notion of integration, the mere notion, was cause for ridicule and punishment. Integration was (1) a remote blip on the screen of the white abolitionist movement, (2) an eccentric afterthought of a small number of Blacks and (3) a political weapon used by white northerners to control white southerners immediately after the Civil War. Integration is equivalent to an idea that was never imagined, a fetus that was never conceived, and the basis of a virtual political reality called Reconstruction. Reconstruction went up in smoke in 1877, as it was supposed to do, and integration went up in smoke along with it. But thousands of exasperated Black individuals, who felt they had nowhere else to call home and nothing else to hold on to, grabbed a handful of that smoke and refused to let it go.

As soon as Black People garner the strength to open their hands and see that nothing is there, We can begin struggling within a different context. We can begin struggling within the context of Black Nationalism. Within that context We can resolve all of the complexes that are driving Us to the nuthouse. Within that context We can become "normal" again.

Final Words

Maybe the resolution of what is discussed in this book is in Nature's hands. Maybe when people talk about values like justice, equality, and fraternity, and of caring for future generations, maybe we are getting a bit ahead of ourselves or, perhaps, assigning ourselves a degree of relevance that is beyond what Nature has bestowed us? If all of the human schizophrenia, destruction and chaos is part of Nature's scheme of things and the moral declarations of human beings are much ado about nothing, then I can resign myself to the hand of fate. But what if Nature is leaving human beings to their own wits? In that case, how will Black People emerge somewhat in tact from their unequal and colonized condition?

I am reminded of one of the oldest tenets of African religious philosophy; that yes, there is a God, but God does not get involved in the affairs of human beings. If God does not get involved, whose responsibility is it to look out for those who have been ruthlessly exploited and victimized and do not have the wherewithal to excel at the power game? Could it be that no one is responsible? Could it be that, in the overall scheme of things, the quality of life of human beings is not that big a deal?

I might be wrong but I think that, 100 years ago people like W. E. B. DuBois, Marcus Garvey and William Monroe Trotter were concerned about the quality of life of Black People today. I think David Walker was concerned about the quality of life of Black People today. I think Mentuhotep II, more than 4200 years ago, was concerned about the quality of life of Black People today, and I think each of them dedicated a lot of their time to making today as safe as possible for those of Us who are here.

There are some present-day Jose Leonardo Chirinos, Toussaint L'Ouvertures, Ann Nzinghas, Tshaka Zulus, Harriet Tubmans and Antonio Maceos hanging out on street corners, carrying out licit and illicit business transactions, studying for exams and preparing for job interviews. They are strong enough and resourceful enough to stop white power in its tracks, separate and enable Black People to take control of Black People's destiny. In the same way some Blacks who would now be more than 500 years old were trying to make today as good as possible for Us, some of today's Blacks will act in a way that is good for generations of future Blacks. They are going to err on the side of caution. They are not going to rely on the traditional enemies of Black People to determine Black People's fate, and future generations of Black People will try to imagine what motivated Us today and be grateful that We were concerned about their welfare.

Mba Mbulu, 2018

9 781982 965426